DYI Stock and Securities Investing

Also Available by Keith Dorney

Becoming Financially Independent
book series

Best Debt Elimination Plan *Debt Management Strategies that Get You Out of Debt Quickly and Economically*

A Beginners Guide to Roth IRAs and 401(k)-Type Plans: *Contribution, Conversion, and Withdrawal Strategies for Building Tax-Free Wealth*

DIY Stock and Securities Investing: *Investment Strategies for Building Wealth and Attaining Financial Independence*

The Bus List—Essential Estate Planning: *Including Wills, Trusts, Durable Powers, Beneficiary Deeds, TODs and PODs, Estate Taxes, Plus Organizing and Securing Your Records*

DIY Stock and Securities Investing

Investment Strategies for Building Wealth and Attaining Financial Independence

Keith Dorney CFP® MA

https://keithdorney.com

Disclaimer:

The information contained within this book is not and should not be construed as financial or investment advice: Advice can only be given once an advisor has a deeper understanding of an individual's complete financial situation. The information in this book should be considered of a general educational nature, not financial or investment advice.

This book will educate you with what is hoped to be correct and up-to-date information, but no warranty or promise is made that everything is 100% accurate.

This book is published as a print-on-demand book for a reason: I update it every year. I take pride in providing only the most up-to-date information in easy-to-understand language.

Table of Contents

For a *Detailed Table of Contents*, see page 239

Do It Yourself?

I don't want to manage your stock investments. I want to teach you how to do it. I want to educate and motivate you to practice only the best stock investing principles.

It's never too early—or too late—to learn how to build one's wealth through stock and securities investing. My strategies will serve you well regardless of your age or stage in life.

There are many paths you can take to build wealth. The one I teach investment-wise is among the easiest to replicate. You don't need special talents, other than your newfound stock investing and money management skills, and it doesn't take years to master.

Your new skills will empower you to pursue financial goals that will make tremendous, positive differences in your life and the ones you love. When saved and invested properly, money can do that:

- Financial independence

- Retirement

- Homeownership

- Peace of mind

- Higher education

- Travel

- ? ? ?

Don't Trust Wall Street

Wall Street wants you to think stock investing is extremely complicated, rocket science if you will. If you listen to "Wall Street," as I collectively refer to the financial services industry, you're doomed to failure or held back at best.

Of course, exceptions exist. There are a handful of investment firms that check all my required boxes. And I know financial planners and investment advisors that provide excellent money management advice for a fair price, but they're few and far between.

As a Certified Financial Planner® who owes a fiduciary duty to clients, I'm embarrassed by Wall Street's behavior. Their primary objective is to make the most money possible off you. There's no higher duty offered or given.

Through bloated expense ratios, advisor and account fees, misleading advertising, and more, they're always looking for a bigger slice, as I document here. They don't have your best interests at heart.

No one cares about your money more than you do. Take control. It may be a lot easier than you think.

Why Listen to Me?

Through my research and that of others, I've discovered the best ways to invest in the stock market. I incorporate these same strategies in the money I manage, as do other managers and informed individuals. I sincerely believe what you're about to read gives you the best chance of success.

I've also come to realize not everyone is as obsessed with stock investing and financial independence as I am. The "why" behind my strategies may be less important than getting started now. Still, others aren't making a move until every strategy is thoroughly explained and understood. I respect those views too and hope to accommodate all.

Whether you're a newbie stock investor who doesn't know an expense ratio from a brokerage fee or a seasoned veteran, follow my *5 Tenets of*

Successful Stock Investing, page 15. They will ensure optimal returns, whatever your level of expertise.

If you're a novice, just want to "set it and forget it," or feel your time is better spent elsewhere, my *One-Stop-Shop Investment Plan (page 62)* could be your solution. It's the simplest of plans yet yields results that will help you realize your financial dreams sooner.

Those of you who enjoy *Getting More Involved (page 73)* read on. Learn how to take a bigger role in the management of your stock investing plan by incorporating individual securities, alternative investments, and more active management.

Some information in this book changes from year to year, like contribution limits, AGI schedules, and other information subject to yearly inflation adjustments. I update this book yearly, so you can be assured you're getting only the latest information.

Still, these limits and schedules will be outdated next year. Make sure you stay informed on those and other changes in the years to come.

That's the kind of thing I write about in my free *Best Money Newsletter*, which publishes just once monthly on the Full Moon. I'll pass along any updates, zone in on a particular money topic, and try and keep it light and breezy. And you can get to know me better in the *Musings from the Tick Farm* section.

Sign-up at *https://keithdorney.com*.

As you get to know me better through my writing, I hope you'll begin to trust what I have to say about stock investing over what Wall Street preaches. In my humble opinion, your financial future depends on it.

Debt Elimination First

Hopefully, I've got you a little fired up about your financial future and what is possible through stock investing. At the risk of deflating that enthusiasm, you may need to take care of something before you begin to build your wealth in earnest.

It's best to be debt-free; However, carrying debt can sometimes be helpful, like using leverage to purchase a long-term real estate investment or personal residence. Other times it can be out of necessity, like for tuition, medical expenses, or rent.

Whatever the reason, address your unwanted debt immediately and above all else. Tackle that debt head-on and with extreme prejudice. Investing any new money in the stock market needs to be temporarily put on hold until that debt is eliminated.

You might have already read my book on eliminating debt. *Best Debt Elimination Plan* is, after all, book 1 of my *Becoming Financially Independent* book series, of which this book is a part. You'll never reach financial independence carrying around high-interest debt, which is why I recommend getting started with that book before this one.

Why do I call my debt elimination plan the "best" plan?

My plan rids you of any unwanted debt in the least amount of time and does it at the lowest cost possible. At least, that's my definition of "best" when it comes to eliminating debt.

Once you get rid of that unwanted debt, pick up where you left off here and resume your wealth-building with a vengeance!

5 Tenets of Successful Stock Investing

I've identified five key stock investing tenets that all stock investors should follow. Follow these fundamentals no matter how you ultimately decide to construct and manage your stock investing plan.

Tenet #1: Minimize Investing Expenses

There has been a revolution of sorts against high stock investing costs as of late. Still, there are plenty of rip-off artists disguised in suits out there ready to take your money. Don't let them fool you. Keeping your investment expenses as low as you can is fundamental to your investing success.

Seek out funds with the lowest of the low expense ratios. Use a brokerage that doesn't charge you a fee when trading individual stocks and ETFs. Be your own best money manager and make your own investment decisions. These actions help keep your investing expenses to the bare minimum.

Passive versus Active Investing

I love and trust my wife and editor of 38 years. I've always leaned on her for sage advice, and she's not shy about voicing her honest opinion. And damn it is she good at Scrabble!

I like to make big splashes and show off my vocabulary with my Scrabble® moves, like getting a triple word score with an obscure word. Meanwhile, Katherine scores well turn after turn with consistent above-average scores while I'm left scrambling. When it's all over, guess who usually wins?

Passive investing is a lot like Katherine's Scrabble style. You may not realize the best return every year, but a consistent return near the top year in and year out wins.

It's not that active management doesn't work. There are active fund and portfolio managers every year who beat their benchmark indexes. The problem is repeating that stellar performance year after year after year.

Much like my Scrabble game, it's tough for that active manager to produce another big score next year. And then the year after. The odds are strongly against it. The odds of a well-managed index fund equaling the performance of its benchmark over the next two years and beyond, however, is practically a given.

A big reason passive investing works is the very low cost of investment. It's something active managers can't ever match. Thanks to fintech and robot efficiency, a handful of companies are offering funds that not only have ever-lower expense ratios but replicate their benchmark index with ever-increasing accuracy.

Having low expenses helps the performance of actively managed funds too. Research shows that the few actively managed funds that did beat their benchmarks accomplished that feat in large part by limiting their expenses: A large majority of those top performers were in the bottom 25% expense ratio-wise.

So, regardless of your investing philosophy — all active, all passive, or a combination — keeping your investing expenses low gives you the best chance of success.

Don't be Average

I think it's human nature to be anathema to average. A large part of Wall Street would like you to think that's what you get when you invest in an index fund, but index funds are anything but. Those companies comprising the indexes didn't get elected as members for being average.

They beat the odds and hundreds of companies

like them to get on that index. And if their performance starts to wane? They're kicked off it. There's no following a stock down to a zero valuation like you can holding an individual stock.

Still, the reason index funds should be a part of your investment plan is their superior performance. Being a lifelong investor and of an age when passive investments didn't exist, I too have had to wean myself off an all-actively managed investment plan. You need to do the same.

I was in the habit of using indexes as a way of evaluating my active investing approach anyway, so index funds have always been on my radar. Once those passive investment products became more efficient and low-cost, I gradually transitioned.

I still own actively managed mutual funds and individual stocks in the money I manage, but indexed ETFs make up the majority. I'd have more active investments if my research indicated otherwise, but it doesn't.

It's up to you. Help subsidize your broker's Tesla® payment with those high expense ratios, brokerage fees, and silly account charges. Or invest that extra capital for yourself and reach your financial goals sooner.

Invest via "Funds"

For the vast majority, make "funds" your ownership choice. It's the best way to employ my risk management strategies, keep your investing costs low, and manage things going forward.

Only use funds that check all the following boxes:

- ✓ No Loads or Brokerage Fees – There is no charge to buy, sell, or exchange. In the mutual fund world, that fee is referred to as a load. When trading ETFs it's a brokerage charge.

- ✓ Meet or Beat Benchmarks – Try and meet or beat all the benchmark indexes that comprise the dynamic diversification of your stock investing plan. This may sound complicated, but I'll show you how easy it can be to do it with passively managed funds. It's all dependent on how much time you're willing to spend managing your plan. Beating even a single benchmark can be time-consuming and hard to do.

- ✓ Lowest Expense Ratios – This is a good time to be a funds investor. Good old capitalism is benefiting both passive and active investors alike. Thanks to technology, competition, and I'd like to think authors like me, expense ratios keep moving lower. Seek out the lowest of the low expense ratios.

The ownership options I recommend not only offer low expense ratios but are the only expenses you incur. Anything extra like a brokerage charge, load, account fee, or the dreaded 12b-1 needs to be avoided like the coronavirus.

As I've been saying, it's a dog-eat-dog world out there on Wall Street. Some charge exorbitant prices in exchange for sub-par returns. A very small segment does it for a fraction of the cost with far superior results.

There are only two types of funds I recommend: No-load mutual funds and brokerage-free exchange-traded funds.

Mutual Funds

There are all kinds of mutual funds out there. For example, if you decide to follow the *One-Stop-Shop Investment Plan*, introduced later, you'll be looking for a single all-in-one no-load index mutual fund that matches your risk tolerance for investment.

The managers of these all-in-ones choose multiple mutual funds to come up with an investment plan for you. That's why an all-in-one is often referred to as "a fund of funds."

If you choose to follow the advice offered in the *Getting More Involved* section, it's you who makes the decisions on the makeup of your investment plan. You can choose from not only multiple mutual funds, but ETFs, individual stocks, and alternative investments too.

You can tell right away if you're dealing with an actively managed or index mutual fund — the index fund often has the word "index" in its title while an actively managed fund won't.

Most websites have filters where you can search for index or actively managed funds under "Management Style" or a similar moniker. Read the prospectus so you're crystal clear as to a fund's investment objective, including what index it's competing with or attempting to replicate.

A mutual fund trades at its *net asset value* (NAV). NAV is calculated once a day, shortly *after* the close of the stock market, and reflects the closing prices of the securities within.

When placing an order to buy or sell a mutual

fund during trading hours, your trade uses the closing NAV determined later that day as your transaction price. Place a trade after that determination, the closing NAV of the next trading day is used.

This burden of having to calculate the NAV every trading day, along with other regulatory reporting requirements, is one reason why mutual funds are losing ground to their brokerage industry equivalent, the exchange-traded fund.

Exchange-Traded Funds (ETFs)

ETFs have different objectives and invest in all kinds of things. I most love the passively managed ones whose only objective is to replicate their benchmark index as accurately and inexpensively as possible.

Take iShares S&P 500 ETF (IVV). This fund currently has an expense ratio of .03 and an r squared of 100%. If you're looking for large-cap domestic equity exposure on both the growth and value side, this would be an excellent choice.

A .03 expense ratio means you're being charged three one-hundredths of one percent of your average yearly balance or around $30 per $100,000 in investment fees. Again, that's a great rate as I write this, but I hope it's headed even lower.

A 100% r squared means the fund duplicates the S&P 500 index exactly. Your return will mirror that of the index, minus investing expenses.

Like individual stocks, ETFs are priced, bought, and sold during trading hours. This used to be a big disadvantage when trading ETFs: Unlike a no-load mutual fund, you had to pay a brokerage commission every time you transacted.

That's not the case anymore, at least with the investment companies I mention here, as well as a growing list of others. ETFs can be traded without a brokerage charge and very well may offer a lower expense ratio than a comparable index mutual fund. That's why everything else being equal, ETFs have become my number one investing vehicle of choice when available.

If you're from the mutual fund world and new to trading ETFs, it may seem at first a bit more complicated to trade than mutual funds. It's not that hard and worth the small learning curve.

Still, there are other considerations when deciding which of the two investment vehicles is the best fit for you.

ETFs vs Mutual Funds

- Mutual funds offer options to automatically reinvest distributed earnings (dividends, capital gains, and interest). ETF earnings are paid in cash and must be manually reinvested.

- As of this writing, all-in-one funds are almost exclusively set up as mutual funds. So, if you're looking for an all-in-one for goals like financial independence and retirement, mutual funds are the only game in town.

- Most 401(k)-type plans don't currently offer ETFs as an affordable option, but I suspect that will change too. In the meantime, your best tax-advantaged option may only offer mutual funds.

- An ETF's minimum investment is the cost of a single share. Some mutual funds have lofty minimum investment requirements, making it more difficult to diversify a smaller portfolio.

- Because ETFs trade like individual stocks, useful trading tools like stops, limits, and stop limits can be utilized. No comparable options exist when transacting mutual funds.

- Some ETFs can delay most or all your capital gains tax until the ETF is sold, while mutual fund earnings by law must be distributed each year and taxed at the investor level. This tax deferment is especially important when investing in regular taxable accounts.

Expense Ratio Explained

Whether you decide to use an all-in-one or multiple funds and ETFs, the expense ratio(s) of the fund(s) you choose equals your cost of investment. That's why you need to know all about expense ratios.

I've stated this previously, but it bears repeating: Seek out no-load funds. No-load funds don't charge you fees other than the expense ratio. It's your only investment expense. Brokerage charges, sales loads, 12b-1 fees, account charges, and redemption and exchange fees need to be avoided.

Expense ratios can be tricky to understand because you're not billed or charged for them like you are for most expenses.

When funds incur expenses, like a management fee, it's reimbursed from the fund. This reduces the fund's net asset value. Think of these expenses as being "built in." They're included in the share price of the fund.

The expense ratio is expressed as a yearly percentage. To calculate what you're being charged in currency, you'd have to compute your average yearly balance and multiply it by the ratio.

Even what looks like a minute difference in expense ratio can add up to a lot of money, especially over time. For example, compare the .05% expense ratio of an index fund to the .75% expense ratio of an actively managed fund, both with a $500,000 average yearly balance.

Remember, since the expense ratio is expressed as a percentage, you need to move the decimal point of the expense ratio two spaces to the left before multiplying. Here's the math:

- index fund: .0005*500,000 = 250.00

- actively managed fund: .0075*500,000 = 3,750.00

- 3,750-250 = **$3,500 difference**

The difference represents how much the active manager must overperform, year in and year out, just to break even with the index fund. That's probably not going to happen.

When totaling the expenses of an investment plan when using more than one fund, don't just add up the expense ratios and multiply your average daily balance by that value. You need to account for each fund as a percentage of assets.

A tallying of total investment plan costs can be helpful when trying to decide on an all-in-one fund versus a plan with multiple funds. For example, assume your investment plan consists of the following four funds:

Fund Name	Expense Ratio	% of Assets
S&P 500 Index	.05	30%
Small-Mid Cap	.07	20%
Total XUS International	.09	10%
Total US Bond	.06	40%

Total year investment expenses are not .27% (.05+.07+.09+.06). The proper calculation, which considers each investment as a percentage of total assets, yields .062%. That's a big difference:

$$(.05*.30) + (.07*.20) + (.09*.10) + (.06*.40) = \textbf{.062\%}$$

One more confusing note about expense ratios.

The expense ratio you're paying may be different from someone else's expense ratio for the same fund, issued by the same investment company. It has everything to do with affiliation.

For example, if you're looking for an aggressive all-in-one index fund for a retirement goal, Vanguard's 2050 Target Retirement mutual fund (VFIFX) is a good choice.

As of this writing (it changes as time moves forward), it has a 90% risky to 10% not-so-risky ratio and a .08% expense ratio.

That's a low expense ratio for an all-in-one, and again it is as of this writing. These days that's about as low an expense ratio as you can find for this type of fund as an individual.

When advising employees of Fortune 150 companies, I'd see 401(k)-type plans offering that same Vanguard® fund with an expense ratio much lower than .08%. What gives?

It's economies of scale. Vanguard® is going to offer a group of tens of thousands of employees a better deal than just you alone. So, if you want the best investment accounts available, find a job with one of those mega-corps (or the federal government) that can swing a much sweeter deal than you can with the investment companies.

Where to Invest

When investing for longer-term goals, it's best to look to your employer's 401(k)-type plan first. Reasons include higher contribution limits, potentially more desirable options due to economies of scale, and any match that may be offered.

If your employer picks the wrong investment company to act as your custodian, however, you could end up paying a lot more in investment fees. Worse, you could get stuck with what I call a dog plan (*https://keithdorney.com/dog-plan*).

Maybe you're not offered a quality plan at work, you're offered no plan at all, or you want to get serious about your wealth-building and deploy multiple tax-advantaged accounts. There are plenty of individual accounts available and it's you who gets to pick the investment company. Following are my favorites:

Vanguard® – The old stalwart still delivers. Love their Admiral index mutual funds and passively managed ETFs. *https://investor.vanguard.com/home*

Blackrock® – Blackrock's iShares® ETFs follow their benchmark index with precision and do it at a low cost. Blackrock is also the custodian of one of my favorite 401(k)-type plans, the federal government's Thrift Savings Account or TSP. *https://www.ishares.com/us*

Fidelity® – They offer a quality Health Savings Account with access to their lineup of mutual funds and ETFs. Fidelity is often the custodian of choice for larger 401(k)-type plans. *https://www.fidelity.com/go/hsa/investing-hsa-your-way*

Other investment companies offer quality products too, and things change, so be sure and shop around.

Tenet #2: Utilize Risk Management Strategies

Risk can never be eliminated from an investment plan. It can, however, be managed. Let me introduce you to three risk management strategies, inspired by *Modern Portfolio Theory*, that should be incorporated into all your investment plans.

These risk management strategies are revisited in more detail later in the *Getting More Involved* chapter. For now, I want you to decide whether to incorporate these strategies yourself or have someone else do it for you. No matter who does it, all three must be done well for optimal results.

Implementing and managing these risk management strategies isn't hard or overly time-consuming, even if you choose to do it yourself. They will help you weather even the most extreme periods of market volatility.

That is unless things go to hell in a handbasket.

Hell in a Handbasket

My Nana used that anachronistic saying all the time whenever things took a negative turn. When I use it, I'm talking about worst-case scenarios, like a large meteor striking Earth, the West Coast of North America falling into the ocean, or a nuclear World War III.

Becoming a refugee also qualifies. My heart goes out to the Ukrainians, the South Sudanese, and countless others displaced by war, famine, and oppression.

All bets are off if any of the above or equivalent catastrophic events happen. Money may be the least of your worries. Sorry for being such a bummer, but the world is crazy and not getting any less so.

Assuming things don't go to hell in a handbasket,

make sure all your investment plans are inoculated with these three risk management strategies. They will serve you well in the future, no matter how you decide to construct your investment plan.

Risk Management Strategy #1

My first strategy has you determine your *risky to not-so-risky ratios* for the coming year as well as all the subsequent years in your investment plan. Decide beforehand how risky you want your plan to be, based on both time horizon and risk tolerance. Make these decisions on your risk level before you invest.

This is done by setting a percentage for both sides of this ratio for each year of the investment plan. Start with year one. On the risky side are your stock investments and any other risky investments. On the not-so-risky side are bonds and other less-risky investments.

The longer your time horizon and the higher your risk tolerance for investing, the closer you want to be to the riskiest of all ratios, a 100-0 risky to not-so-risky ratio. The shorter your time horizon and the lower your risk tolerance for investing, the closer you want to be to a 0-100 risky to not-so-risky ratio.

Your investment plan should never have a riskier ratio in the next year than you had the year before: Your ratio should either stay the same or shift to less risky. This is due to your ever-decreasing time horizon for investment and should be true regardless of your risk tolerance.

By choosing to invest in an all-in-one fund, as discussed in the upcoming *One-Stop-Shop Investment Plan*, you're hiring your custodian to come up with those ratios for you. The problem with the all-in-ones is that only the time horizon is considered. I want you to consider your risk tolerance for investment too when devising your plan, whether you're choosing an all-in-one or building your own.

Risk Management Strategy #2

Once you've determined your risky to not-so-risky ratios for all the years of your investment plan, it's time to construct what I call your *dynamic diversification*. Do this for both the risky and not-so-risky sides.

This task is greatly simplified by using no-load mutual funds and trade-free ETFs. Hundreds of top-performing companies can be bought with a single fund. Use multiple funds, and you can achieve levels of diversification not possible with individual holdings.

On the risky side, you want to mix small, medium, and large company stocks, along with stocks with different investment styles (value and growth) into the plan. When longer time horizons exist, international stocks should also be a part of this diversity.

On the not-so-risky side, which consists of fixed-income investments like bonds, interest rate risk and business risk exist. Interest rate risk is managed by investing in short-, medium-, and long-term investments, while the business risk is managed by investing in fixed-income investments that have varying degrees of business risk.

The "dynamic" element of dynamic diversification refers to how your diversity changes from year to year, on both sides of the ratio. Just as your risky to not-so-risky ratios get more conservative over time, so should your diversity.

Investments with higher levels of both business and interest rate risk are shunned on the not-so-risky side in place of more conservative less-risky investments. Same on the risky side. The riskier elements on this side like international and small-cap stocks are gradually given up in place of less risky ones.

Once again, choose your level of involvement. Pay the custodian of your chosen all-in-one fund to devise your dynamic diversification for you both now and in the future, or you can do it yourself.

Risk Management Strategy #3

My third and last risk management strategy concerns the ongoing management of your just-created investment plan, which I call *rebalancing and reassessing*.

At least once a year, investment plans need to be rebalanced back to the risk level defined by the plan, which will more than likely get knocked out of whack due to the volatility of the stock market. Eventually, yearly downward adjustments to your risk level must also be made too, per your pre-determined risky to not-so-risky ratios and dynamic diversification.

The reassessing part of this third strategy is reserved for more active investors. Besides making those predetermined changes per your risky to not-so-risky ratio and dynamic diversification, maybe you want to make some other changes?

There are lots of ways to tinker with a passively managed plan, but you don't want to overreact to any goings on either. Still, lots of us can't help but tinker *just a little bit*.

Once again, leave it to the manager of your chosen all-in-one fund to do the rebalancing and reassessing for you, or do it yourself. It's up to you to decide.

Tenet #3: Invest Tax-Advantaged

When investing for longer-term goals like financial independence and retirement, you need to be all-in on tax-advantaged accounts. Why? You're practically guaranteed a higher after-tax rate of return because of the tax advantages.

I advise maxing out all your tax-advantaged opportunities first before even thinking about investing in a regular taxable account. Why not take advantage of the free wealth-building tools your Uncle Sam offers?

Combine those tax savings with high-performing funds with the lowest expense ratios. Then add my three risk management strategies and you've got one of, if not the best wealth-building tools on the planet!

Choosing an Account

There are many tax-advantaged accounts available in the United States. Unfortunately, the rules passed by our legislators and interpretations of those rules by the IRS can be complicated and confusing. That's why I've dedicated a whole chapter, *Tax-Advantaged Accounts (page 165)*, to them with all the details.

I'll offer a quick review of my top three tax-advantaged accounts here from the perspective of where you should look first, based on the utility of each account.

First on my list is any employer-sponsored plan. Most commonly, if you're offered one, it's in the form of a 401(k)-type plan, which includes 401(k), 401(a), 403(b), 457, TSP, and others. I call them 401(k)-type plans because from an employee's standpoint they all have similar rules.

Unfortunately, using your employer's plan can be paradoxical. On the plus side, these plans have much higher yearly contribution limits than other tax-advantaged accounts. The regular contribution maximum for the year 2025 is $23,500, $31,000 if you're age 50 or older.

That's why I had you look for a 401(k)-type plan first. For example, compare those limits with the 2025 IRA contribution limits of $7,000, or $8,000 if you're age 50 or older. It's not even close.

But what if the 401(k)-type plan you're offered comes with bloated expense ratios and nonsensical fees? Unfortunately, some do, and there's not much you can do about it except look for another job. If you want to keep your job despite its lousy plan, think about investing elsewhere if you've got what I call a dog plan (*https://keithdorney.com/dog-*

plan).

Luckily, I've found most employers do a decent job with their 401(k)-type plan offerings. If you're stuck with a dog plan, there are lots of alternative tax-advantaged accounts available. Most are individual accounts where you get to pick the custodian. You're not stuck with the investment firm your employer chose like with 401(k)-type plans.

Next up is a Health Savings Account or HSA (page 200). Personally, this is my favorite because it potentially has four tax advantages, more than any other account. What does that equate to? A higher after-tax rate of return and lots of tax-free cash!

An HSA and the strategies I recommend are not for everyone. However, if you check all the boxes and save it for later in this unique way, you too could become an HSA millionaire!

Maybe you don't have an employer-sponsored plan and an HSA isn't a good fit for you. Never fear. The Roth IRA (page 181) is here!

In my opinion, everyone should have a Roth IRA and stuff it with as much cash as they can. Earnings accrue tax-free in a Roth IRA, making all your later withdrawals tax-free and insulated from future tax hikes.

A Roth IRA is also one of the few tax-advantaged accounts where you can make tax-free withdrawals anytime: You don't need a good reason or be age 59 1/2. I find a lot of folks don't know that. This feature is especially helpful for those of you striving to become financially independent before age 59 1/2.

With many tax-advantaged accounts, including IRAs and most 401(k)-type plans, you're faced with yet another very important question: Should I make traditional or Roth contributions?

Traditional vs Roth

When I go to get a cone at Screamin' Mimi's, my favorite ice cream shop, it doesn't matter what flavor I order. I'm never disappointed.

Whether I go with one of my two standbys, deep dark secret or butter pecan, or with a seasonally fresh masterpiece, it doesn't matter. They're all so good!

When investing in tax-advantaged accounts, look at the traditional vs Roth contribution dilemma the same way. Whichever "flavor" you choose, it's all good. You're getting great tax benefits either way.

However, being flexible and clever with what flavor you contribute each tax year (traditional, Roth, or perhaps a double dip?) can add to your advantage.

A Quick Tax Review

Taxes are deferred on traditional contributions, giving you a tax deduction in the year of the contribution. All distributions, including contributions and accumulated earnings (interest, dividends, and capital gains), are taxable at ordinary income tax rates when you take them out come age 59 1/2 or older.

By law, earnings on Roth contributions accrue tax-free, not tax-deferred like with pre-tax contributions. That means withdrawals on Roth funds at age 59 1/2 and older are 100% tax-free. The catch is you must pay tax, at ordinary income tax rates, on your contributions in the years you make them.

A Case for Traditional Contributions

There are a lot of good reasons for traditional contributions. A shorter-term goal, like accumulating the down payment for a personal residence or getting out of debt, may be paramount to longer-term goals. Remember, traditional contributions maximize your take-home pay when compared to Roth contributions, which means a bigger paycheck and lower taxes.

A higher wage earner may want to maximize traditional contributions to avoid paying tax at the highest brackets, as will anyone who wants more money now, for whatever reason.

A Case for Roth Contributions

When I'm retired and no longer working and earning wages, wouldn't you expect my tax rate to be much lower than it is now? I get asked this question, or a variation thereof, a lot by employees after making my case for at least some Roth contributions.

Expecting lower taxes in retirement may be a tad short-sighted. All distributions from traditional contributions and associated earnings are fully taxable upon withdrawal. So are pensions. Even Social Security payments are taxable up to 85%.

Plus, for folks reaching their mid-70s, *Required Minimum Distributions* (page 193) kick in. If you've done a good job saving for retirement over the years, that RMD can be quite large.

Of course, that extra reported income is accompanied by an extra-large tax bill, especially after it's added to the rest of your income. And that's to say nothing about the government raising tax rates, which seems inevitable.

Do you anticipate generating a bunch of earnings from your contributions? The more earnings you generate, the more motivated you should be to suck it up and go Roth. Young people have long time horizons for investment and can expect large amounts of tax-free earnings. So do savvy investors who expect above-average returns.

And don't worry about that potential tax problem later: *Money in your Roth IRA is exempt from both taxes and RMDs.*

Managing Contributions

Just as with good ice cream, tax-advantaged contributions are delectable no matter the flavor. You'll enjoy a higher after-tax return with either. Still, besides deciding beforehand how much to contribute for the coming year, try and figure out which type(s) of contributions are most advantageous: All traditional contributions, all Roth, or a combination of the two.

Let's say you're in your 50s, at the top of your pay scale at work, have two kids in college, and want to retire soon. Best to make traditional contributions.

That tax deduction is more valuable than ever now that you're in a higher tax bracket. Making a Roth contribution at this point costs you big bucks, which you need to pay for your kids' tuition. Additionally, because you're retiring soon, earnings will be more limited, thus reducing the utility of tax-free earnings.

Instead, say you're age twenty-one and just getting started in the workplace. You'll want to make Roth contributions.

Unless you're a professional athlete or Hollywood movie star, you're probably in a lower tax bracket at this point. It just makes sense to get that tax liability over with while it's so low. Plus, your time horizon for investment is very long, so lots of tax-free earnings can be expected.

Enjoy a Double-Dip
If you're somewhere in between these extremes, or you just can't decide, consider splitting your contribution.

It's easy to split your 401(k)-type plan contribution between traditional and Roth. Even though both contribution types go into the same account, your custodian, the investment company hired by your employer to run their plan, keeps track of associated earnings. When you're ready to

take money out, you'll know what flavor it is—
taxable or non-taxable. In the IRA world, you'll
need two accounts (traditional and Roth) to
double-dip.

Traditional vs Roth contributions? In some years
it's clear-cut which type of contributions to make,
while in others it will be more muddled.
Managing these year-in and year-out decisions
regarding traditional and Roth contributions is
just another way to increase your advantage.

Tenet #4: Make Timely Investments

When I say timely, I'm not advocating market
timing or day trading. Notice how day traders
disappear come a bear market, only to resurface
again when things turn rosy again? Most of us
have better things to do.

What I mean by timely is consistently investing
toward a predetermined goal. You can look for
additional advantages along the way too in the
hopes of boosting your return.

Most Important Money

Spend most of the money you earn as you wish.
That's your business. I'm only concerned about a
sliver of those earnings, that percentage of net
income you take right off the top of every

paycheck.

That's the best way to save and invest for any financial goal: Do it every paycheck.

Even the best stock investing plan with the greatest amount of tax advantages does you no good if you don't have the money to feed it. Call this small fraction of your income saved your prosperity percentage, savings percentage, or whatever. It's your *most important money*.

Before starting any stock investing plan, make sure you're comfortable with your per-paycheck savings rate. Unless you're committed to saving that percentage every paycheck, any plan, no matter the quality, just won't work.

You may want to try your percentage on for size before enacting your plan. Make sure it's realistic. Set yourself up for success, not failure.

This behavior is encouraged by 401(k)-type plans. Just set a percentage for the year and your most important money is taken off the top and invested per your instructions like clockwork.

If you're investing in IRAs instead, or you're employing multiple tax-advantaged accounts, you can follow a similar path. As soon as that paycheck clears your account, off goes your most important money percentage to your chosen custodian and invested per your plan.

Set Your Percentage

Everyone, no matter what their age, income level, or stage in life, should strive to save at the very least a net 10 percent of what they make. If you're serious about your wealth-building, start at 15.

More motivated individuals, higher wage earners, and the thriftier and more frugal among us can save even more—17, 20, 24, 27, or even 30 percent plus.

That's not to say lower-earning folks can't achieve amazing financial goals too. I've witnessed firsthand dozens of inspirational transformations from rags to riches and have read about many more.

What's your definition of rich? Often, it comes down to a matter of perception. What is considered a rag to some is a treasured garment to others, just as what you consider "riches" are baubles to Elon Musk.

Any incremental increase in your savings helps, so don't be hesitant to bump up your percentage by half a percent if you can't afford the whole. Even a quarter-percent jump in your savings rate will make a big difference in the long run.

The next time you get a raise, don't go out and just spend that extra money. Instead, keep your expenses fixed and raise your percentage.

If you haven't been a successful saver so far, it doesn't matter. It's you who controls your financial future. Committing grave financial errors in the past has no bearing on what's going to happen next. Unless you let it.

Are you leaning toward the simplest investment plan possible, my *One-Stop-Shop Investment Plan*? Why not match that simplicity with a savings plan as equally simple and automatic?

Handling Lump Sums

If you're lucky enough to receive an influx of cash, whether from an inheritance, bonus, tax refund, or another source, don't even think about it. Invest it all towards your most important financial goal.

If you're nervous about the market taking a big tumble right after you invest that lump sum, you can dollar cost average that windfall over a given time. For example, divide the lump sum by a year's worth of pay periods, and add that amount to your existing contribution every time you're paid.

Keep in mind history shows that the odds favor investing a lump sum immediately, so make sure there's hard financial data behind your apprehension.

If you're investing for a longer-term goal in tax-advantaged accounts, add that lump sum to your existing contributions. If that lump is larger than your allowed contributions for the year, it might be time to deploy a new tax-advantaged account. Or save the extra for next year's round of contributions.

Tenet #5: Have a Plan

Never invest in stocks without a purpose. If you do, your investment will be much like a rudderless boat: You'll go this way and that and never really get to where you want to go.

Schedule a Meeting

Right now, set aside at least an hour of your time for an important meeting. With yourself. If you have a significant other, invite them to the meeting too.

You're going to make some very important decisions during this meeting, so set it at a time when you'll be at your best and won't be distracted. Keep in mind even a small amount of time spent on financial planning and goal setting pays huge dividends.

Financial Goalsetting

During your financial goalsetting meeting, brainstorm all the things you want to accomplish that require money outside of your budget. Summarize each want into a few words and write them down on paper, an electronic device, or a whiteboard so you can study them.

You hopefully have a goal of financial independence or retirement at or near the top of your list. You don't want to have to work unless you want to in your later years.

Unless you're one of the lucky ones with a cushy pension, nobody is saving for your retirement except you and the Social Security Administration. As you may know, even the modest amount you're due to receive from the SSA may very well be reduced. Unless Congress acts, we're looking at around a 30% reduction, so take your goals of financial independence and retirement seriously.

Decide to be singular in your pursuits or direct your most important money towards several goals. Aim high but be realistic.

Next, consider your savings percentage and the

number of goals on your list. Narrow that list as necessary. Now assign what you feel is a realistic completion date for each goal. It's fine to guess at this point.

Prosperity Paragraphs

From your narrowed list, I suggest expanding those few words describing each goal into a paragraph. Keep it short, no longer than four sentences, and include those projected completion dates. I recommend completing this exercise even if writing isn't your thing.

It's been proven repeatedly that writing down what you're trying to accomplish greatly enhances your chance of achievement, so make sure you don't skip this important step.

As you write, use first-person language, pretending you've already achieved your goal. Try and capture how you'll feel on that magical day with your words.

You're the only one who's going to read these paragraphs. Don't bother about the quality or form. Just make sure it's from the heart.

Write prosperity paragraphs for all your financial wants, even the ones you probably won't be able to afford until later. Writing down and visualizing these less urgent goals helps solidify what's most important and helps with your efficacy.

Ideally, stash your prosperity paragraphs away for a few days, then reread them. It's the ones that send shivers up and down your spine after you read them that you should pursue. You want to spend your most important money on something grand, something that's going to make positive changes in your life and the ones you love.

Prosperity Paragraph Examples

- It's the year 2029. I'm officially done with "Conglomo Corp" as of yesterday with more than ample retirement savings. As I sip my early morning coffee, I know today is a special day, the first day of the best time of my life.

- It's spring 2026 as we pull into what is now our new driveway. Our kids run from the car, through the front entrance, and up to their new rooms: No more bunk beds for those two. It wasn't easy saving the gargantuan sum needed for the down payment and closing costs. But now, smelling lilac as I gaze over the grounds, I know it was worth it.

- I leave the stage to join my family this late

spring day, one and a half years after starting my journey. With my hard-earned degree in hand, I realize all those night school hours were worth it. My immediate jump in pay is nice but in the longer term I know this is just the beginning.

- An incredible weight, one I've been carrying around for far too long, has finally been lifted. It took eleven months and lots of financial discipline to eliminate my unwanted debt, but now the opportunities for the future seem endless.

- The days of waking up and dreading going to work are over. Saving every penny I could scrounge over the last two years gave me the financial cushion I needed to pursue my dream. Now I can't wait to get out of bed and get going on my new business, which can't help but succeed given my newfound work ethic.

Quantifying Your Goals

Once you've completed your prosperity paragraphs it's time to get more realistic. You need to quantify each goal. Specifically, figure out how much of your per paycheck savings it will take to reach each goal by your prescribed dates.

For short-term goals, simply divide the sum needed by the number of pay periods between now and your goal's fruition date. Since we're talking less than 2 years, inflation and your rate of return will be minimal, so including them isn't necessary.

With longer-term goals, including inflation and a rate of return is necessary to get as accurate a forecast as possible. This can be a difficult step for some, especially if you're a bit math challenged. Luckily, technology can come to the rescue. It makes arriving at an accurate estimate much easier.

Turn to an online calculator to do the heavy lifting. The investment companies and custodians I mention here all offer calculators you can use for free. Or check the custodian's website of your employer's 401(k)-type plan for help.

There are lots of other resources available too. The securities and exchange commission offers a savings calculator at *investor.gov* or check out NerdWallet's® version at *https://www.nerdwallet.com/article/finance/savings-goal-calculator/*.

Once you've got some hard numbers, revisit those financial goals. This can be difficult because there's a good chance your savings aren't going to be big enough. You're bound to have to make some adjustments at this point, whether it's lengthening a time horizon, putting off a lesser important goal, or deciding to up your most important money percentage.

Once you've identified what goal or goals you want to pursue, set a timeline for achievement. Calculate the percentage needed for each paycheck for attainment. Now you're ready to devise a customized investment plan for your goal(s).

By now, I hope you're starting to get an idea of where you stand risk-wise. Paramount to building any investment plan, whether that plan consists of a single fund or something more complex, is having a good handle on your own risk tolerance for investment.

Risk Tolerance for Investment

Perhaps you've taken one of those ubiquitous risk tolerance quizzes. Based on your responses to a series of questions, you're labeled conservative, aggressive, or more likely somewhere in between. These assessments can be helpful and may give you some insight into your investing personality.

Sticking to Your Plan

As an individual investor, sticking to your plan as the sky is falling can be hard to do, but your future investing success depends on it! That's why it's so important to incorporate your risk tolerance into any investment plan.

Whether a more conservative portfolio wins out in the future, or stocks continue to outperform is anyone's guess. No one can predict what will happen, but you can construct customized investment plans suitable to both your risk tolerance and time horizon.

Dirty Filthy Money

But there are other variables at work here. How you were raised, psychological hang-ups, and scarcity of money are just a few.

Try and come to grips with your financial past the best you can. And don't beat yourself up regarding past mistakes with money. We've all made them, and they have no bearing on your future success. Unless you let them.

Money is not the root of all evil, nor is it a magic pill that solves all your problems. It's an acquisition tool, an object for trade, and nothing more. An honest assessment of your risk tolerance starts with being more pragmatic about money and leaving your emotions out of it.

Aggressive Investors

I like to describe aggressive investors as those who are most optimistic about the stock market's stellar past repeating. Aggressive investors are willing to stick with stocks and scrape together even more investment capital during the worst downturns. If history repeats, those investments will eventually eclipse their previous highs, just like they always have.

Aggressive investors load up heavily on risky investments from the beginning. They maintain those investments in their plans longer than conservative investors. Still, to succeed they need to apply those same risk management strategies just like everyone else.

Conservative Investors

Conservative investors, on the other hand, aren't as confident and patient. Whether it be irreconcilable bi-partisan politics, war, acts of terrorism, natural catastrophes, climate change, or worldwide pandemics, the conservative investor is more pessimistic regarding the future success of stock and other risky investments.

The lower your tolerance for risk, the more conservative your investment plans need to be. More conservative plans start less risky from the get-go, maintain their more conservative mix throughout, and dump riskier investments sooner than more aggressive investors.

Inflation Risk

The problem with not-so-risky investments is their rate of return. Many of them, because of their relative safety, earn a rate of return below the rate of inflation. That means even though your principal is secure, you're still figuratively losing money because those dollars don't buy what they used to.

That's why even the most conservative among us

need to invest at least some money into risky investments when their time horizon dictates. It's one of the few ways to keep up with inflation and at the very least keep your head above water.

Given this inflation risk, *Modern Portfolio Theory* (page 151) calculates a conservative 100% not-so-risky portfolio as riskier than one that has a small percentage of riskier investments like stock. By now, you've surmised I'm a fan of *Modern Portfolio Theory*. Guilty as charged!

Ultimately, no one knows what combination of investments will prevail and whether a stock-rich portfolio wins as it has in the past. Choose your level of risk carefully, then hang on for the ride.

Risk Tolerance Assessment

Pretend you're age 35 and just implemented your new investment plan for financial independence with an aggressive 85% investment in stocks. Over the next month, there's a steep stock market decline of 40%.

Are you going to leave that investment plan alone and continue to follow it? Are you going to double down and scrounge around for even more capital to invest? Or are you going to bail to try and stop the bleeding?

Losing almost half your savings in the blink of an eye is unthinkable to some. If that's your mindset, reconsider your risky investment percentages accordingly. Another big contraction, whether caused by a bubble, pandemic, war, or some other yet unknown disaster could be right around the corner. Nobody knows for sure.

Having a better understanding of your risk tolerance will help you choose a mix of investments that's right for you. That's true whether you go with the one-stop-shop investment plan or decide to get more involved.

One-Stop-Shop Investment Plan

My one-stop-shop investment plan is one fund within a single tax-advantaged account. And all those necessary risk management strategies are done for you. You can't get much simpler than that! Although simple, it offers better returns at a lower cost than what almost all of Wall Street has to offer.

You can have superior performance and low fees without compromising any of my best investing fundamentals. I'll bet you'll be surprised how easy it can be to check all the necessary boxes.

Your Best Tax-Advantaged Account

If you have a rich uncle who loves you and wants to help you out financially, you'd be crazy to turn down the help, right? I'm not sure your Uncle Sam loves you, but he's willing to help you out money-wise big-time when it comes to boosting your after-tax rate of return.

[Note: When I refer to Uncle Sam, I mean the United States government which makes the laws, and sometimes more specifically the Internal Revenue Service (IRS) which collects the taxes.]

I want you to be all-in on tax-advantaged accounts for all your medium and longer-term goals like financial independence, education, and retirement. Keep in mind these accounts are not suitable for short-term and shorter medium-term goals, as most come with withdrawal restrictions.

In the spirit of this chapter's theme of one-stop-shopping and simplicity, there's also a lot less paperwork to do in a tax-advantaged account when compared to a regular taxable one come tax time. There's no need to keep track of the basis of your contributions nor your reinvested dividends, capital gains, and interest when investing in a tax-advantaged account.

That's because distributions of Roth money are tax-free, and traditional withdrawals are taxed at your future ordinary income tax rate. The basis for those liquidated investments is not needed in either case.

Somewhere out there is your own best tax-advantaged account. It's the one that gives you the most tax advantages, has high yearly contribution limits, and hopefully offers low-cost all-in-one funds.

Maybe your best tax-advantaged account is the 401(k)-type plan offered by your employer. Again,

I suggest looking there first because these accounts have much higher contribution limits than individual tax-advantaged accounts.

For 2025, the regular contribution limit is $23,500, $31,000 if you're age 50 or older. That's compared to the 2025 IRA contribution limits of $7,000 and $8,000 respectively.

If your employer offers you a match, you simply must take full advantage of it, no matter the state of your employer's plan. If you don't, you're working for free part of the time. Both Uncle Sam and your employer view it as part of your compensation and you should too.

Ideally, your employer's plan offers low-cost funds and thoughtful all-in-one options. Otherwise, you may need to look elsewhere.

If you're still confused about where to turn, open a Roth IRA at Vanguard®, assuming you're under the Roth IRA income limits (page 181). Invest in one of their all-in-one target index mutual funds. Pick the one that's most appropriate (see below). In my opinion, everyone should have a Roth IRA.

If you live in the United States, there are plenty more great tax-advantaged accounts out there besides a Roth IRA and your employer's plan. My personal favorite is the Health Saving Account, but traditional IRAs, 529s, and others could have a place in your investment plans too. Check them out, along with all the details, in *Tax-Advantaged Accounts* (page 165).

Find the Index Funds

Don't let Wall Street, or even Vanguard® for that matter, fool you into investing in actively managed funds. Only invest in an actively managed fund if it's been clobbering its benchmark. Skip right to the index funds. For the one-stop-shop investment plan, look for all-in-one index funds, which go by a few different names:

- Target Funds

- Lifecycle Funds

- Target Retirement Funds

- Freedom Funds

These funds are set up as "funds of funds." The target fund's investment plan is comprised of multiple individual index funds that represent the manager's desired risk and diversity options.

You'll find the breakdown of these investment plans in the prospectuses of the all-in-one funds. If you've got an employer-sponsored plan, your employer has those prospectuses available, usually on the custodian's website.

Read the Prospectus

By law, pertinent information must be disclosed in a similar format inside a fund's prospectus. The powers that be, in the United States that's the Securities and Exchange Commission, ensure companies can't fool you with misleading information in their prospectuses as they may do in their advertising.

Look for the index funds with dates in the title, like the 2055 Target Retirement or the 2035 Freedom Fund. First, open the prospectus for the fund whose date most closely corresponds to your projected withdrawal date. Find the investment percentages, what I call your dynamic diversification. Next, compute the risky to not-so-risky ratio for the first year of the plan.

Many all-in-ones use stock and bond index funds exclusively in their plan's composition, making it easy to tally your risky to not-so-risky ratios. Add up the percentages of the different stock investments—that's your risky-side percentage. Do the same for the bond investments and mark them on the not-so-risky side.

Other all-in-ones may use real estate, commodities, and even crypto investments in addition to stocks on the risky side. Alternative not-so-risky investments, like CDs, money markets, and ultra-shorts may be utilized too. Add up the percentages, put them on the correct side, and make sure the two percentages add up to a hundred.

As an example, I'll use the US government's version of the 401(k)-type plan, which Uncle Sam calls the Thrift Savings Plan or TSP. Up-to-date information on the TSP can be found at *tsp.gov*.

By the way, the TSP is a fantastic plan. Compare your plan's index all-in-one expense ratios versus the TSPs if you dare. They're the lowest of the low. Uncle Sam got the TSP right. If you have access to the TSP, you're lucky to have it. Be sure to take advantage.

Don't Follow the Instructions

These all-in-one funds, including the TSP's, come with instructions. They say to estimate your retirement or target date, the day you want to start withdrawals, then choose the appropriate target fund that has that date (or close to it) in its title. This fund, calculated using birthdates and assuming a normal retirement age, is often the default choice for participants in 401(k)-type plans.

Unfortunately, following those instructions or going with the company's default choice can be disastrous. The manager of your supposedly appropriate all-in-one might have a vastly different definition of risk than you.

Choosing your default could prove to be too risky: You won't stick to the plan when the going gets crazy. Or your default choice may prove to be not risky enough, causing you to lose patience with a lower return.

Lie About Your Age

As of this writing, the TSP offers nine index all-in-ones, which they call Lifecycle Funds, in increments of five years from 2025 to 2065. Each of the nine plans uses the other five index funds offered by the plan, the G, F, C, S, and I fund, in various combinations. G and F are not-so-risky funds, and C, S, and I are risky funds.

The following are the TSP's risky to not-so-risky ratios for all their Lifecycle Funds. This data was copied from their website, tsp.gov, in June of 2023. Make a similar chart for the index all-in-ones that you're offered:

Fund Name	Risky %	Not-So-Risky %
~~Income~~	25	75
~~2025~~	37	63
~~2030~~	60	40
~~2035~~	66	34
~~2040~~	72	28
~~2045~~	77	23
~~2050~~	82	18
~~2055~~	99	01
~~2060~~	99	01
~~2065~~	99	01

Notice the first fund listed is the TSP's Income Fund, also known as the L funds. When any of the Lifestyle Funds reach the last year of their investment plan, money is transferred from the Lifestyle Fund's final year investment mix to the Income Fund, where a 25% risky to 75% not-so-risky ratio is maintained. As you should expect, the Income Fund has the least risky ratios of all the TSP's Lifecycle Funds.

I crossed out the target dates under the fund name for a reason. I want you to choose the appropriate fund based on the current risky to not-so-risky ratio rather than your projected target date.

As an example, say you're age 40 and a very conservative investor. By default, you're shoved into the 2050 fund. Do you really want 82% of your current investments invested in stock and other risky investments? If your risk tolerance for investment is low, an 82-18 mix is probably way too risky. Look to the 2045, 2040, or 2035 funds for a more agreeable ratio instead. That's what I mean by lying about your age.

On the other hand, maybe you're age 40 and have a super-aggressive risk tolerance. An even more aggressive mix may be sought versus the default 2050 option. Look to the 2055, 2060, and 2065 funds.

Please remember these numbers are as of this writing. For up-to-date information on the TSP, visit *tsp.gov*.

Put on Autopilot

Once you've chosen the perfect all-in-one fund, be sure and put all your money in that single fund and have future contributions go there too. One more thing. Be sure all the earnings generated by the fund (interest, dividends, and capital gains) are reinvested to buy more shares.

The manager of your chosen all-in-one will incorporate all those necessary risk management strategies for you. They'll set up your risky to not-so-risky ratios for now and in the future, determine your dynamic diversification on both sides of the ratio, and take care of any ongoing management issues, including rebalancing and reassessing.

After you've got everything set up, keep feeding that super-charged beast of an investment plan more money. That's all you need to do.

Even if you're sure you want to go with an all-in-one fund, skim through the following *Getting More Involved* sections. You're bound to pick up a few tips that will help you be a better stock investor.

Also, be sure and read more about your chosen account(s) and look for other accounts you may qualify for in the *Tax-Advantaged Accounts* chapter (page 165). Get better informed about Uncle Sam's sometimes confusing rules governing your chosen accounts. There may be potentially life-changing features allowed by these accounts, some of which you may not be aware of.

Getting More Involved

There are lots of reasons to shun the all-in-ones and take over the management of your investment plan:

- Include shares of your company's stock

- Introduce more active management through individual shares and/or actively managed funds

- Incorporate alternative investments including real estate, commodities, derivatives, and digital assets

Many enjoy managing and schedule that necessary time commitment into their busy schedules. Again, it's not rocket science, but those risk management strategies don't manage themselves. If your interest is limited, do yourself a favor and stick with an appropriate all-in-one fund.

Revisit the Prospectus

In the prospectuses of the all-in-one funds referenced in the *One-Stop-Shop Investment Plan* chapter, there is a wealth of information. If you recall, I asked you to find the risky to not-so-risky ratios for the all-in-one funds in those prospectuses, either at your employer's website or at Vanguard®.

If you study the prospectuses of different target all-in-one funds as I do, you'll find it easy to spy the risky to not-so-risky ratios not only for the first year of the plan but for the year after too. In fact, you'll find the investment mixes for every year of the plan, through the target date and the distribution period too.

You'll also see a breakdown by percentage of how both sides of the ratio will be invested, what I call your dynamic diversification. On the risky side, you'll see large, medium, and small-cap stock investment percentages and a bit of international. There may be alternative investments thrown in there too.

On the not-so-risky side there will be short, intermediate, and longer-term bond investments, as well as ones with varying degrees of business risk. Alternative fixed income investments may be part of the mix too.

After you get through a few of these prospectuses, you'll see professional managers have varying opinions on what your investment plan should look like for a particular time horizon. You may also start to get a sense of what your own numbers should look like, both for now and in the future.

See for yourself. On most investment company websites, you don't need to be a customer or even leave an email address to access a prospectus. Studying how professional managers are doing it is a good start on your way to managing your plan more actively.

For example, you don't need to be a federal employee, serviceman, or servicewoman to see what the Thrift Savings Plan (TSP) managers at Blackrock® recommend in their Lifecycle Funds. Nor do you need to be a customer to check out the Indexed Target Retirement Funds at Vanguard®.

Even though those managers may disagree on how risky a plan should be, one thing they do agree on is using investing principles derived from Modern Portfolio Theory (MPT). Like me, they follow key MPT fundamentals because they work.

Benchmark Indexes

Be sure you have a good understanding of benchmark indexes and how to use them to evaluate performance. They're important regardless of your investment philosophy.

Find the True Benchmark

Root out the true benchmark index in a fund's prospectus using r squared. You'll usually find several indexes in a prospectus that are used for comparison: Find the one with the r squared closest to 100%. That's your true benchmark index. Ignore the others.

As an example, say your fund's true benchmark is the S&P 500 Index®. Standard and Poor's, now a part of S&P Global®, is the keeper of one of the most closely followed indexes in the world, which follows the performance of the large-cap US equities market.

Research prices of your US large cap holdings year to date as well as 1, 3, 5, 7, and 10 years. Next, search for the closing price of the benchmark index for those same dates and compare.

Does the fund consistently beat its benchmark, or is it lagging? Don't settle for even a little negative disparity. A small lag makes a big difference in your return when added up year after year, especially when investing for medium and longer-term goals.

For individual securities, categorize your holdings by market cap and investing style and track the most applicable index. Compare your overall and individual stock performances against those benchmarks.

For example, say your portfolio of large-cap US investments includes individual shares of Disney® (DIS), Microsoft® (MSFT), Molson Coors Brewing Company® (TAP), Meta Platforms® (FB), as well as dozens of other large-cap US stocks. You could use the S&P 500 as a barometer for overall performance, but a more accurate assessment would be to break it down further by using a large growth and a large value index.

Assign DIS, TAP, and the other large value stocks a large value index like CRSP US Large Value. Same with MSFT, FB, and the other large US growth stocks in the portfolio: Use a large growth index like CRSP US Large Growth.

Remember to be honest with yourself. Don't fall in love with a stock and keep it even though your research and tracking indicate otherwise.

If your large-cap holdings consistently lag the indexes, why bother? Split up your US large-cap money and invest in VUG and VTV, large-cap growth and large-cap value funds respectively. Or blend your large growth and value investments into VOO or IVV, two S&P 500 ETFs, and forget about that segment of your diversification until your rebalancing and reassessing date.

Do this evaluation for all areas of your dynamic diversification. There are not-so-risky benchmarks you can follow too, so it's easy to compare performance on both sides of your ratio.

The Substitute Index Caper

Compare the return of your current actively managed mutual fund, ETF, or stock portfolio to the investment's *true* benchmark index. I italicize "true" because that's a caper many Wall Streeters try and pull: Comparing their return to a similar but lesser-fit index that makes them look better.

Do the returns of your actively managed fund consistently lag its true benchmark index? You have an easy way to answer that question, and it's not reading the investment company's misleading advertising.

Stock Indexes

There is a plethora of stock, bond, and sector indexes maintained by a variety of institutions. The following represents but a portion of the index universe.

Try searching for your benchmark indexes by name in your app's search feature. If your app doesn't support indexes, find one that does.

As an alternative, you can track an ETF that follows the index instead. Make sure the ETF has an r squared of 100% or 1, as do the previously mentioned ETFs from Vanguard® and Blackrock®. 100% or 1 represents exact correlation with the index, making it a suitable substitute benchmark.

Some ETFs, like traditional indexes, follow a particular market cap, investing style, or both. Other ETFs follow specific economic sectors. You can probably find an appropriate ETF that closely follows even the most obscure of your actively managed risky and not-so-risky investments.

S&P Global®

The folks at the conglomerate now known as S&P Global® maintain many US and international indexes and is home to two of the most popular ones, the Dow Jones Industrial Average and S&P 500:

S&P Global®		
S&P 500	US Large-Cap	Both large-cap growth and value in one index
S&P MidCap 400	US Mid-Cap	Both mid-cap growth and value in one index
S&P SmallCap 600	US Small-Cap	Both small-cap growth and value in one index
S&P Composite 1500	US Small, Mid, & Large	Includes stocks in the S&P 500, 400, and 600
S&P Global 1200	All Regions of the World	Over 30 countries and 70% of world markets
S&P International 700	World Minus US	S&P 1200 minus the S&P 500
Dow Jones Industrial	30 US Industrial Corp.	Price-weighted index not cap-weighted like most

CRSP®

The quants at the University of Chicago would love for you to use their CRSP (Center for Research in Security Prices) indexes to compare performance by investment style and market cap:

CRSP®	
Mega Cap Growth	Largest Growth stocks in the US
Mega Cap Value	Largest Value stocks in the US
Mid Cap Growth	US Mid-Cap Growth
Mid Cap Value	US Mid-Cap Value
Small Cap Growth	US Small-Cap Growth
Small Cap Value	US Small-Cap Value

FTSE Russell®

The consolidation of index holders is prevalent on both sides of the pond. The London Stock

Getting More Involved

Exchange Group® owns what is now known as FTSE Russell®, a collection of popular US and international indexes:

FTSE Russell®		
Russell 3000®	US Stocks	The 3,000 largest US companies (97% of US market)
Russell 3000® Growth	US Growth	The growth element of the Russel 3000
Russell 3000® Value	US Value	The value element of the Russel 3000
Russell 1000®	US Large Cap	The 1,000 largest companies in Russell 3000
Russell 1000® Growth	US Large Growth	The growth element of the Russell 1000
Russell 1000® Value	US Large Value	The value element of the Russel 1000
Russell 2000®	US Small Cap	The 2,000 smallest companies in Russell 3000
Russell 2000® Growth	US Small Growth	The growth element of the Russell 2000
Russell 2000® Value	US Small Value	The value element of the Russell 2000

Other Major Indexes	
NASDAQ Composite®	A blend of most all the companies listed on the tech-heavy NASDAQ Stock Exchange
NASDAQ 100®	The 100 largest technology (non-financial) companies listed on the broader NASDAQ Composite
MS EAFE®	Major world markets minus the United States and Canada

Risk Management Strategies

If you've been reading sequentially, you're already familiar with the three risk management strategies I recommend you apply to all your investment plans:

1. Risky to Not-So-Risky Ratios

2. Dynamic Diversification

3. Rebalancing and Reassessing

In this chapter, you'll learn how to implement and manage these risk management strategies yourself rather than have someone else do it for you like with an all-in-one fund. Your end game is to boost returns by building customized investment plans for all your financial goals.

Risky to Not-So-Risky Ratio

It's your time horizon for investment and risk tolerance that dictates your ideal risky to not-so-risky ratios for both now and in the future. That's why proper ratios should vary from investor to investor, even when they have the same time horizon.

Because of your ever-decreasing time horizon for investment, your risky to not-so-risky ratio needs to change over its lifetime. Specifically, from risky to less risky. That's true whether your risk tolerance is super-aggressive, ultra-conservative, or somewhere in between.

That way, if a big stock market downturn

coincides with your goal's fruition date, it doesn't affect you as much. By that time your money has transitioned to ultra-conservative not-so-risky investments, which are the most impervious to market volatility.

Increasing the percentages of your not-so-risky investments and subsequently decreasing the risky side as your target date approaches should be fundamental to all your investment plans.

The First Year
The first step in creating your investment plan is to determine your risky to not-so-risky ratio for year one. Assuming your time horizon is more than one year, this ratio should be risky. It should be the riskiest (or tied for the riskiest) of all the years in the plan. This is true regardless of your risk tolerance.

Every year that goes by, that's one less year on your time horizon. Long-term goals eventually become intermediate, intermediate goals eventually turn short-term.

That's why *you never want to have a more aggressive plan next year than you had the year before*. You either want to keep the risk level the same or decrease it.

The Last Year
The last year of your plan, the year you liquidate

some or all your investments, should be the least risky of all the years in your plan, excluding any distribution years. Whether this last year contains risky investments or not is dependent on the length of any distribution period.

In-Between Years

Once you have the first and last years' ratios, it's easier to fill in the in-between years. Year by year, gradually switch from risky to less risky by adding to the less risky side and trimming the risky. Try and make it a smooth transition by gradually switching over.

Distribution Periods

The length of any distribution period must also be considered in your ratios:

- **No Distribution Period** – If there is no distribution period, both conservative and aggressive investors should have a 0%-100% risky to not-so-risky ratio for the last year.

- **Longer Distribution Periods** – The longer the distribution period, the bigger your riskier percentage should be for that last year. Examples: Retirement, financial independence, full-time higher education, or any other goal where the distribution period is more than one year.

Come up with numbers you're comfortable with for both now and in the future. The following examples illustrate appropriate numbers for an ultra-conservative and super-aggressive investor respectively: More than likely your own ideal numbers lie somewhere in between these extremes.

Risky to Not-So-Risky Ratio Example #1
In example #1, you're creating an investment plan for a short-term goal of two years. Examples could include saving for the down payment on a house, establishing an emergency reserve fund, or taking an expensive vacation. Unless you're investing money you can afford to lose, better to stick with an all-not-so-risky portfolio (0-100) for both years one and year two, regardless of your risk tolerance.

In one or two years, anything can happen stock-market-wise. Don't diversify and you've taken on even more risk. Yes, you could hit a home run. Or you could strike out and lose all your money.

That's why I recommend shunning stock and other risky investments with a two-year or less time horizon despite your risk tolerance, assuming your goal has no distribution period.

Plan Year ~ Conservative Ratio ~ Aggressive Ratio

1 ~ 0-100 ~ 0-100

2 ~ 0-100 ~ 0-100

Your rate of return won't be exceedingly high in these two years, but you can rest assured that your financial goal is going to be achieved without a hitch.

Risky to Not-So-Risky Ratio Example #2

Assume now you're pursuing a college savings goal for your 8-year-old. That gives you a 10-year time horizon in which to invest, along with a 4-year distribution period. Both conservative and aggressive investors can now afford to invest in risky investments like stock. Of course, aggressive investors will be more stock-heavy throughout and conservative investors more bond-heavy.

As with any financial goal, the first step in creating your customized investment plan is determining what your risky to not-so-risky ratio is going to be for plan year one. In this example, that's the first year of a ten-year investment plan followed by a four-year distribution period.

Plan Year ~ Conservative Ratio ~ Aggressive Ratio

1 ~ 25-75 ~ 75-25

Your second step is coming up with ratios for the last year of the plan, the year before the start of the four-year distribution period, which is plan year 10.

Plan Year ~ Conservative Ratio ~ Aggressive Ratio

10 ~ 0-100 ~ 25-75

Next, fill the in-between years 2-9.

Plan Year ~ Conservative Ratio ~ Aggressive Ratio

1 ~ 25-75 ~ 75-25

2 ~ 23-77 ~ 70-30

3 ~ 21-79 ~ 65-35

4 ~ 18-82 ~ 60-40

5 ~ 15-85 ~ 50-50

6 ~ 12-88 ~ 45-55

7 ~ 9-91 ~ 40-60

8 ~ 6-94 ~ 35-65

9 ~ 3-97 ~ 30-70

10 ~ 0-100 ~ 25-75

Finally, determine ratios for the four distribution

years, which I call plan years 11-14.

Plan Year ~ Conservative Ratio ~ Aggressive Ratio

11~ 0-100 ~ 20-80

12 ~ 0-100 ~ 10-90

13 ~ 0-100 ~ 5-95

14 ~ 0-100 ~ 0-100

Risky to Not-So-Risky Ratio Example #3

This example looks at risky to not-so-risky ratios for a longer-term goal of retirement in 25 years.

Assuming the stock market performs anything like it has in the past, this is your opportunity to make some real money. If you have even longer to invest for retirement, that's even better. This is true for both conservative and aggressive investors since both sets of ratios will be more stock-heavy than the previous examples.

Once again, these ratios represent two investment extremes: ultra-conservative and super-aggressive. Most likely your ideal ratios—the ones you'll stick with through thick and thin—lie somewhere in between.

Begin by determining your risky to not-so-risky ratio for plan year 1, which would be 25 years before your projected retirement date.

Plan Year ~ Conservative Ratio ~ Aggressive Ratio

1 ~ 70-30 ~ 99-1

Next, set your ratio for plan year 25, the last year before your projected retirement date.

Plan Year ~ Conservative Ratio ~ Aggressive Ratio

25 ~ 25-75 ~ 65-35

Finally, fill in the in-between plan years 2-24. Remember to gradually make the transition from plan year 1 to plan year 25.

1 ~ 70-30 ~ 99-1

2 ~ 68-32 ~ 99-1

3 ~ 66-34 ~ 98-2

4 ~ 64-36 ~ 98-2

5 ~ 62-24 ~ 96-4

6 ~ 60-40 ~ 94-6

7 ~ 58-42 ~ 92-8

8 ~ 56-44 ~ 90-10

9 ~ 54-46 ~ 88-12

10 ~ 52-44 ~ 86-14

11 ~ 50-50 ~ 84-16

12 ~ 48-52 ~ 82-18

13 ~ 46-54 ~ 80-20

14 ~ 44-56 ~ 79-21

15 ~ 42-58 ~ 78-22

16 ~ 40-60 ~ 77-23

17 ~ 38-62 ~ 76-24

18 ~ 36-64 ~ 75-25

19 ~ 34-66 ~ 74-26

20 ~ 32-68 ~ 73-27

21~ 30-70 ~ 72-28

22 ~ 29-71~ 70-30

23 ~ 27-73 ~ 68-32

24 ~ 26-74 ~ 66-34

25 ~ 25-75 ~ 65-35 (retirement date)

When I'm customizing an investment plan for a longer-term goal, I always fill in the distribution years, but with this caveat. 25 years is a long time.

By the time your retirement date rolls around, circumstances may have changed. Maybe you have more money than you need or not enough. And who knows what the world will look like in the year 2050?

That's what the reassessing part of the third and final risk management strategy, rebalancing and reassessing, is for. Even though your ratios may change, I still recommend you fill in the risky to not-so-risky ratios for all the years of your plan, including the distribution years, before you invest another penny.

Add the distribution years, which I call plan years 26-40.

Plan Year ~ Conservative Ratio ~ Aggressive Ratio

26 ~ 24-76 ~ 65-35

27 ~ 24-76 ~ 65-35

28 ~ 23-77 ~ 64-36

29 ~ 23-77 ~ 63-37

30 ~ 22-78 ~ 62-38

31 ~ 21-79 ~ 61-39

32 ~ 20-80 ~ 60-40

33 ~ 20-80 ~ 60-40

34 ~ 20-80 ~ 60-40

35 ~ 20-80 ~ 60-40

36 ~ 20-80 ~ 60-40

37 ~ 20-80 ~ 60-40

38 ~ 20-80 ~ 60-40

39 ~ 20-80 ~ 60-40

40 ~ 20-80 ~ 60-40

Dynamic Diversification-Risky Side

As I write this, it's the dog days of summer, and sports-wise major league baseball is the only game in town through my narrow view of sports. While I wait for the start of the football season, allow me a baseball analogy.

Even the big hitters can't afford to swing for the fences every at-bat. If they did, it wouldn't be long before they're swinging for the River Cats, IronPigs, or Lug Nuts in the minors.

The best hitters pick their spots. They know they can better help their team by getting on base rather than striking out a lot, a byproduct of swinging for the fences.

These days batters know through analytics it may be long odds to try and hit a home run off a particular pitcher, especially when he throws a particular pitch. So, they wait. They make the pitcher work, and only when "it's time" do they take that mighty swing. For other at-bats, it makes more sense to ease up and aim for that huge opening in left-center or even take pitches to get on base.

If you invest in just one very risky stock, you could hit a home run and get a great return. If you strike out, however, you could lose most if not all your money. If you can't afford to lose that money, better ease up a bit on that swing and, depending on your risk tolerance, try hitting for a single, double, or triple instead.

By spreading your risk around to different areas of the "park," your batting average (as well as your investment plan) will perform much better in the long run.

Because of their stellar past performance, stocks will comprise a large part if not all the risky side of things for most investors. Keep in mind the terms "stock" and "equities" are often used interchangeably in Wall Street's parlance.

Diversification on the risky side of your ratio

means including different types of stocks and other risky investments with varying degrees of risk. Dynamic diversification means gradually shifting the riskiest parts of your risky side to less risky investments before crossing over to the not-so-risky side.

Risky investments have different degrees of risk. An emerging market international investment or a small-cap domestic stock is way riskier than an S&P 500 index fund, for example. It's not that you can't lose money with that S&P 500 index fund. You can still lose your shirt. However, with those riskier investments, you could lose your shirt *and* your pants.

Market Cap

One way to diversify is to own different size companies. Best to mix it up and purchase companies that are worth lots and lots of money, others not so much, and everything in between.

Market capitalization, or market cap, is a fancy phrase for the market value of a company. Find the market cap for any company by multiplying the number of shares outstanding by its current stock price. It depends on whom you talk to as far as what connotates small, medium, or large these days, but what's a few billion among friends?

Market Capitalization	
Small Cap	Less than 3 Billion
Mid Cap	3-12 Billion
Large Cap	Over 12 Billion

Invest in all different sizes. Small companies are riskier but can yield higher returns. Larger companies are generally less volatile than medium and small companies but may have a smaller upside.

Even if you invest solely in large-cap stocks, you're still in the stock market and your money is subject to substantial risk. Again, we're talking about different degrees of risk here.

More conservative investors will gravitate more towards less volatile large-cap stocks when diversifying. Contrarily, more aggressive investors will favor more volatile small and medium-cap companies and a bigger international element.

Growth versus Value

Determining whether a stock is growth or value is often referred to as finding the stock's investing style. Value stocks include companies that are considered "undervalued" in the marketplace and generally pay higher dividends, while growth stocks pay little or no dividends but have greater appreciation potential.

Technically speaking, the difference between growth and value is rather hollow. Is not the potential growth of a company a component of value and vice versa? Still, I find the distinction, however muddled, helpful when diversifying.

There's a formula used to determine the investment style of a stock, which includes quantifying price/earnings and price/book ratios, among other measures. It's much easier, however, to let technology do the heavy lifting for you by relying on your chosen app or search engine to determine the investing style of an investment for you.

Domestically, load up around 50-50 on value and growth stocks. I say that because historically, a blended portfolio of value and growth has performed better than exclusively growth or value.

It makes sense to include both in your diversity. This is especially true when investing in tax-advantaged accounts, where you don't have to worry about year-to-year tax liability.

Each year, of course, there's a clear winner. Sometimes growth stocks hammer value, often for consecutive years on end. At other times it's the opposite. Trying to predict which will do the best next year and favoring one investment style over another is one way to manage your investment plan more actively, which can have both rewards and perils.

The Morningstar® Box

Sleek, informative, and elegant, the Morningstar® Equity Style Box is a simple yet effective tool that instantly communicates a fund's objectives regarding market cap and investing style. Draw a square, then delineate that square into nine smaller squares:

large-cap value	large-cap blend	large-cap growth
mid-cap value	mid-cap blend	mid-cap growth
small-cap value	small-cap blend	small-cap growth

The three vertical squares, from bottom to top, represent market cap: small, medium, and large. The three horizontal squares from right to left represent investing style: growth, blend, and value.

You'll see just one square blackened for most funds, informing you where that fund would potentially fit into your investment plan. With other funds, a broader reach is represented by the blurring of two or more squares.

I'm not the only one who calls for a 50-50 split between value and growth. Lots of fund managers invest equally in both investment styles for a particular market cap, thus earning one of the three blended middle squares in the Morningstar® box. This is true for both passive and active fund managers.

International Stocks
Diversifying to an even greater extent can be accomplished by investing internationally. Of course, many great companies exist all over the world. Just remember investing internationally, no matter where you call home, exposes you to double jeopardy.

Not only are you betting on the performance of that foreign company, but also on how your country's currency does versus the country's currency in which you're investing.

For example, a US resident investing in a biotech company in Switzerland does so with Swiss francs. During their holding period, the return could have as much to do with the performance of the company as with the exchange rate between the dollar and franc, as francs are returned to dollars when the stock is sold. International stocks sold on domestic exchanges are also affected by this same currency risk.

Individual Stocks

If individual stocks are a part of your investment plans, much research and ongoing management are necessary. Unless you're willing to become an expert on those corporations in your portfolio and follow them daily, it's best to stick with funds.

Although investing in any stock is considered risky, some stocks are much riskier than others. For example, a large value stock like The Walt Disney Company® (DIS) is much less volatile than Splunk® (SPLK), a small growth company.

You can make or lose a ton of money investing in either, but the volatility of SPLK is much greater than DIS, who is much larger, more diversified, and has been around the block a time or two.

A big advantage of holding individual securities is control. You choose when to buy and sell, your level of activity, and when to incur taxes if your holdings are in a non-Roth account. With other methods of ownership, those decisions are often made for you and without your best interests necessarily in mind.

However, unless you're in the business, properly managing a diversified portfolio of individual securities is arduous if not impossible. Keep in mind that when I say diversified, I'm talking about a minimum of 40 stocks, ideally many more.

When I say daily, I mean keeping up with developments from all your individual stock holdings every day. That's what's necessary since breaking news on one of your holdings may require immediate action on your part.

Be honest when asking yourself the following questions:

- How much time in my busy schedule can I devote to investing?

- Am I able to follow the markets daily?

Your Company's Stock

What about acquiring the stock of your employer? Many corporations award employees shares of company stock as part of their compensation. In addition, an ESPP or similar discount equity purchase plan may be offered.

Certainly, following the goings-on within your own company may be doable. There's also something to be said for being both an employee and a part-owner. Still, be honest as to whether that stock warrants a place in your investment plans.

If you decide to keep some or all your acquired company stock, attach it to a specific financial goal. Always invest with purpose.

It's also crucial you understand where those stocks stand as far as market cap and investing style. Assign them the proper diversification classification and liquidate other investments in that classification as necessary to make room for them per your predetermined percentages that make up your dynamic diversification.

For example, say you work for a medium-cap growth company and want to include your company's holdings in your investment plan. Any other mid-cap growth investments, like mid-cap growth mutual funds and ETFs, would have to be reduced to make room for those individual shares. The same goes for any other individual stock holdings you want to include in your plan.

Although it can be difficult, be honest with yourself about your company stock and its place in your investment plan. The last thing you want is to follow your company stock down the proverbial rabbit hole. You don't want to be out of a job *and* broke.

Actively Managed Mutual Funds

An actively managed mutual fund manager aims to beat the performance of the fund's benchmark index. This is done through an "active" management approach, which involves a lot more buying and selling than if passively managed. This results in more investment fees and a higher expense ratio.

Some actively managed fund families not only have high expense ratios but brokerage fees for buying and selling funds, early redemption fees, account fees, 12b-1s, and others. Why folks invest in these funds is beyond me.

The problem with most actively managed mutual funds is they perform at a level below their benchmark index once those expenses are subtracted. Over a ten-year period, actively managed funds investing in US large- and mid-cap stocks underperformed their benchmark index

97% of the time. For actively managed US small-cap stock funds, managers underperformed 77% of the time.

The likelihood of one of those successful active managers repeating their stellar performance again the following year is 20%. In year three, the chances of overperforming once again drop to just 10%. Remember, these percentages are of the original 3% (or 23% if investing in small-cap) who overperformed in year one, which makes for a very small group going forward.

These types of statistics can be misleading, as any time frame can be used to satisfy an author's hypothesis. As stressed in the *Find the True Benchmark* chapter, I recommend you do your own research going forward.

Are there mutual funds that clobber their benchmark year after year? From the statistics, you can see they are few and far between. But if you can identify one for even just a part of your dynamic diversification, it could prove to be a boon to your overall return.

Some investment companies talk a good game. They publish misleading information about performance and claim superiority in their advertising, but all the while are woefully underperforming.

Only if a fund is consistently outperforming its benchmark do you want it in your portfolio. Otherwise, it's a fool's game chasing around that best return year after year.

Commodities

You can use commodity futures, commodity stocks, ETFs, and mutual funds to invest in agricultural products, energy, metals, livestock, and meat. Historically, commodity markets have proven to be more volatile than the stock market.

Much attention is paid to the precious metals markets, especially gold. Like any highly volatile investment, if you're going to include it in your investment plan, incorporate it using these risk management strategies and make it a sliver, not a slice.

Derivatives

Derivatives include forwards, futures, options, and swaps. Some allow you to bet on a stock or index going down. Loaning money on margin is involved in this "shorting," which amplifies gains and losses more than just the change in stock price.

My risk management strategies strive to reduce your overall risk when investing. Amplifying risk using derivatives is counter to that objective.

Cryptocurrencies

As an author, educator, and CFP®, I get to talk with lots of investors. More and more of you are trading cryptocurrency, investing in crypto futures, buying non-fungible tokens, and otherwise embracing digital assets as a mainstream investment.

So, if you're already investing in it, you've got lots of company. If you're not investing in it, it's time to take notice. Just keep in mind crypto is a super-volatile investment.

If you follow the spot price of Bitcoin and Ethereum like I do, you know what extreme volatility looks like. BTC and ETH are almost always at the top of my watch list, whether for the biggest percent gainer or loser.

I have more traditional highly volatile investments on my watch list too, including small growth stocks, a small value index, and an international pharmaceutical company. BTC and ETH usually beat them too volatility-wise, making crypto the riskiest of the risky as far as investments go.

That's exactly what you're looking for when you want to hit a home run with an investment: High volatility. These are the investments with the largest percentage gaps in their 52-week high/lows and the highest standard deviations.

You could double, even triple your money in a hurry investing in crypto. But what's your next move? Try and do it again? Somewhere down the line, given crypto's extreme volatility, you're going to end up on the wrong side. So, what's the best way to invest?

Remember my baseball analogy at the beginning of this chapter? If you invest all your money in crypto, you could hit a home run and get a great return. You also could strike out and lose most if not all your money.

If you can't afford to lose all your money, better to ease up a bit on that swing. Depending on your risk tolerance for investing, try hitting at the appropriate times for a single, double, or triple as well as those home runs.

What percentage you invest in crypto has everything to do with your time horizon as well as your risk tolerance for investment. The longer your time horizon and the higher your risk tolerance, the bigger you can afford your crypto percentage to be.

Like with any super-volatile investment, it's best to take a long-term approach. That means *holding on for dear life* through the crazy ups and downs you're sure to experience with the riskiest of the risky.

Keeping your investing expenses low is my number #1 tenet of successful investing. Unfortunately, that's not easy to do right now with crypto. Highly inefficient and high-fee investment vehicles are the norm. There's also the issue of security, especially if you trade crypto via a "hot" digital wallet.

Just as it was in the early days of mutual funds, when expense ratios were 5% instead of .05, it's Wall Street who's making the lion's share of the profits these days. I'm waiting for products to come along that offer more affordable ways to invest in crypto.

There are a few crypto-based ETFs, but they are inefficient, expensive, and potentially even more volatile than the spot price they're following. Take BITO from ProShares®. They invest in crypto futures, meaning your losses can be amplified, and performance can differ from the cryptocurrency you're betting on.

Grayscale Investments® and others offer trusts

that track cryptocurrencies and are designed to trade like stocks. These vehicles, like expense-bloated actively managed stock mutual funds and REITs, violate my tenet #1 too. They are inefficient and cost you big time in return for their convenience and liquidity.

If you're going to trade crypto, let me offer some advice. First off, don't "trade" crypto. I'll bet neither Stephan Curry nor Tom Brady, two sports celebs who are "seen trading crypto" on commercials for a now bankrupt company, actively trades crypto. That's just Wall Street trying to deceive you and raise their profits.

If you're going to invest in crypto, it's best to be a "hodler" and have a plan. Buy your coin directly through a reputable cryptocurrency exchange and consider offline storage. If you insist on a hot wallet, make sure your broker practices 2-factor authentication and takes security seriously.

Wall Street Real Estate
Wall Street has devised ways for you to invest in real estate without getting your fingernails dirty. Properties are bundled into an investment trust (REIT), mutual fund, or ETF, and split up and sold as shares of equity.

You don't get all the tax benefits associated with

direct real estate investing; however, you do enjoy liquidity. Assuming sufficient trading volume exists, which isn't a problem except for the smallest of issues, you can sell your shares from your computer or smartphone in an instant.

With these ownership options, everything is on autopilot for you the investor, but know that you'll pay, sometimes dearly, for those services. High management and investment fees are the norms.

Another potential problem with Wall Street real estate is taxes. By law, the lion's share of income generated by these ownership options must be distributed and taxed in the year it occurred.

That income and subsequent tax liability are split up among shareholders, and tax must be paid in the year that it occurred, even if you hadn't liquidated any shares. That's why it's best to invest in Wall Street real estate in a tax-advantaged account versus a regular taxable one.

You may already be invested in REITs and similar real estate investments through your holdings. For example, the S&P 500 index's makeup includes around a 3% real estate share.

Dynamic Transition

Dynamic diversification allows you to participate and benefit from any meteoric rise in your riskiest investments, but be OK if things go in the other direction. That's the dynamic part of dynamic diversification. It's still all about managing your risk.

A portion of your diversified investment plan will be aiming for the fences, positioned in the riskiest of the risky. This is where your small-cap stocks and similarly volatile investments fit. Other parts of the risky side will be invested in other risky investments with less volatility and risk.

The dynamic element of your dynamic diversification gradually shifts your portfolio out of those home run-type investments and into those that are less risky, without yet crossing over to the not-so-risky side. We're talking about different degrees of risk. Once your time horizon shrinks to just a few years, riskier investments are no longer a part of the plan.

That's the dynamic part of dynamic diversification at work: It shifts your investment plan over time to less risky investments, ensuring a soft landing come your financial goal's fruition.

The following examples build on the three from

the previous *Risky to Not-So-Risky Ratio* chapter. Examples 1-3 depict the same short, medium, and long-term goals respectively, along with the same risky to not-so-risky ratios used previously. Remember, your ideal numbers more than likely lie somewhere in-between the two extremes (ultra-conservative and super-aggressive) depicted in the examples.

Diversification-Risky Side Example #1

Example #1, if you recall, is a short-term goal of 2 years. As you can see, the risky to not-so-risky ratios for an ultra-conservative and super-aggressive portfolio are the same:

Investing Year ~ Conservative Ratio ~ Aggressive Ratio

1 ~ 0-100 ~ 0-100

2 ~ 0-100 ~ 0-100

There are no risky investments in either the conservative or aggressive ratios, leaving nothing to diversify.

Diversification-Risky Side Example #2

Example #2 is a medium-term educational goal of 10 years (for an 8-year-old) with a 4-year distribution period.

Plan Year ~ Conservative Ratio ~ Aggressive Ratio: Dynamic Diversification

1 ~ **25**-75 ~ **75**-25: **Conservative investor** – 25% risky: 18% US large cap, 5% US mid-small cap, 2% international ~ **Aggressive investor** – 75% risky: 30% US large cap, 30% US mid-small cap, 15% international

2 ~ **23**-77 ~ **70**-30: **Conservative investor** – 23% risky: 18% US large cap, 4% US mid-small cap, 1% international ~ **Aggressive investor** – 70% risky: 30% US large cap, 28% US mid-small cap, 12% international

3 ~ **21**-79 ~ **65**-35: **Conservative investor** – 21% risky: 18% US large cap, 3% US mid-small cap ~ **Aggressive investor** – 65% risky: 30% US large cap, 25% US mid-small cap, 10% international

4 ~ **18**-82 ~ **60**-40: **Conservative investor** – 18% risky: 16% US large cap, 2% US mid-small cap ~ **Aggressive investor** – 60% risky: 30% US large cap, 23% US mid-small cap, 7% international

5 ~ **15**-85 ~ **50**-50: **Conservative investor** – 15% risky: 15% US large cap ~ **Aggressive investor** – 50% risky: 30% US large cap, 18% US mid-small cap, 2% international

6 ~ **12**-88 ~ **45**-55: **Conservative investor** – 12%

risky: 12% US large cap ~ **Aggressive investor** – 45% risky: 30% US large cap, 15% US mid-small cap

7 ~ **9**-91 ~ **40**-60: **Conservative investor** – 9% risky: 9% US large cap - **Aggressive investor** – 40% risky: 30% US large cap, 10% US mid-small cap

8 ~ **6**-94 ~ **35**-65: **Conservative investor** – 6% risky: 6% US large cap ~ **Aggressive investor** – 35% risky: 30% US large cap, 5% US mid-small cap

9 ~ **3**-97 ~ **30**-70: **Conservative investor** – 3% risky: 3% US large cap ~ **Aggressive investor** – 30% risky: 30% US large cap

10 ~ **0**-100 ~ **25**-75: **Conservative investor** – 0% risky ~ **Aggressive investor** – 25% risky: 25% US large cap

off to college

Plan Year ~ Conservative Ratio ~ Aggressive Ratio: Dynamic Diversification

11 ~ **0**-*100* ~ **20**-*80:* **Conservative investor** – 0% risky ~ **Aggressive investor** – 20% risky: 20% US large cap

12 ~ **0**-100 ~ **10**-90: **Conservative investor** – 0% risky ~ **Aggressive investor** – 10% risky: 10% US

large cap

13 ~ **0**-100 ~ **5**-95: **Conservative investor** – 0% risky ~ **Aggressive investor** – 5% risky: 5% US large cap

14 ~ **0**-100 ~ **0**-100: **Conservative investor** – 0% risky ~ **Aggressive investor** – 0% risky

Diversification-Risky Side Example #3

Example #3, if you recall, was a long-term retirement goal of 25 years. The risky to not-so-risky ratios and dynamic diversification for an ultra-conservative and super-aggressive portfolio are as follows:

Plan Year ~ Conservative Ratio ~ Aggressive Ratio: Dynamic Diversification

1 ~ **70**-30 ~ **99**-1: **Conservative investor** – 70% risky: 40% US large cap, 15% US mid-small cap, 15% international ~ **Aggressive investor** – 99% risky: 39% US large cap, 30% US mid-small cap, 30% international

2 ~ **68**-32 ~ **99**-1: **Conservative investor** – 68% risky: 40% US large cap, 14% US mid-small cap, 14% international ~ **Aggressive investor** – 99% risky: 39% US large cap, 30% US mid-small cap, 30% international

3 ~ **66**-34 ~ **98**-2: **Conservative investor** – 66% risky: 40% US large cap, 14% US mid-small cap, 12% international ~ **Aggressive investor** – 98% risky: 39% US large cap, 30% US mid-small cap, 29% international

4 ~ **64**-36 ~ **98**-2: **Conservative investor** – 64% risky: 40% US large cap, 13% US mid-small cap, 11% international ~ **Aggressive investor** – 98% risky: 39% US large cap, 30% US mid-small cap, 29% international

5 ~ **62**-24 ~ **96**-4: **Conservative investor** – 62% risky: 40% US large cap, 12% US mid-small cap, 10% international ~ **Aggressive investor** – 96% risky: 39% US large cap, 30% US mid-small cap, 27% international

6 ~ **60**-40 ~ **94**-6: **Conservative investor** – 60% risky: 40% US large cap, 12% US mid-small cap, 8% international ~ **Aggressive investor** – 94% risky: 39% US large cap, 29% US mid-small cap, 26% international

7 ~ **58**-42 ~ **92**-8: **Conservative investor** – 58% risky: 40% US large cap, 11% US mid-small cap, 7% international ~ **Aggressive investor** – 92% risky: 39% US large cap, 29% US mid-small cap, 24% international

8 ~ **56**-44 ~ **90**-10: **Conservative investor** – 56% risky: 40% US large cap, 10% US mid-small cap, 6% international ~ **Aggressive investor** – 90% risky: 39% US large cap, 29% US mid-small cap, 22% international

9 ~ **54**-46 ~ **88**-12: **Conservative investor** – 54% risky: 40% US large cap, 10% US mid-small cap, 4% international ~ **Aggressive investor** – 88% risky: 39% US large cap, 29% US mid-small cap, 20% international

10 ~ **52**-44 ~ **86**-14: **Conservative investor** – 52% risky: 40% US large cap, 10% US mid-small cap, 2% international ~ **Aggressive investor** – 86% risky: 39% US large cap, 29% US mid-small cap, 18% international

11 ~ **50**-50 ~ **84**-16: **Conservative investor** – 50% risky: 40% US large cap, 9% US mid-small cap 1% international ~ **Aggressive investor** – 84% risky: 39% US large cap, 28% US mid-small cap, 17% international

12 ~ **48**-52 ~ **82**-18: **Conservative investor** – 48% risky: 40% US large cap, 8% US mid-small cap ~ **Aggressive investor** – 82% risky: 39% US large cap, 28% US mid-small cap, 15% international

13 ~ **46**-54 ~ **80**-20: **Conservative investor** – 46%

risky: 40% US large cap, 6% US mid-small cap ~ **Aggressive investor** – 80% risky: 39% US large cap, 27% US mid-small cap, 14% international

14 ~ **44**-56 ~ **79**-21: **Conservative investor** – 44% risky: 40% US large cap, 4% US mid-small cap ~ **Aggressive investor** – 79% risky: 39% US large cap, 27% US mid-small cap, 13% international

15 ~ **42**-58 ~ **78**-22: **Conservative investor** – 42% risky: 40% US large cap, 2% US mid-small cap ~ **Aggressive investor** – 78% risky: 39% US large cap, 27% US mid-small cap, 12% international

16 ~ **40**-60 ~ **77**-23: **Conservative investor** – 40% risky: 40% US large cap ~ **Aggressive investor** – 77% risky: 39% US large cap, 27% US mid-small cap, 11% international

17 ~ **38**-62 ~ **76**-24: **Conservative investor** – 38% risky: 38% US large cap ~ **Aggressive investor** – 76% risky: 39% US large cap, 27% US mid-small cap, 10% international

18 ~ **36**-64 ~ **75**-25: **Conservative investor** – 36% risky: 36% US large cap ~ **Aggressive investor** – 75% risky: 39% US large cap, 26% US mid-small cap, 10% international

19 ~ **34**-66 ~ **74**-26: **Conservative investor** – 34% risky: 34% US large cap ~ **Aggressive investor** –

74% risky: 39% US large cap, 26% US mid-small cap, 9% international

20 ~ **32**-68 ~ **73**-27: **Conservative investor** – 32% risky: 32% US large cap ~ Aggressive investor – 73% risky: 39% US large cap, 26% US mid-small cap, 8% international

21~ **30**-70 ~ **72**-28: **Conservative investor** – 30% risky: 30% US large cap ~ Aggressive investor – 72% risky: 39% US large cap, 25% US mid-small cap, 8% international

22 ~ **29**-71~ **70**-30: **Conservative investor** – 29% risky: 29% US large cap ~ **Aggressive investor** – 70% risky: 39% US large cap, 23% US mid-small cap, 8% international

23 ~ **27**-73 ~ **68**-32: **Conservative investor** – 27% risky: 27% US large cap ~ **Aggressive investor** – 68% risky: 39% US large cap, 21% US mid-small cap, 8% international

24 ~ **26**-74 ~ **66**-34: **Conservative investor** – 26% risky: 26% US large cap ~ **Aggressive investor** – 66% risky: 39% US large cap, 19% US mid-small cap, 8% international

25 ~ **25**-75 ~ **65**-35: **Conservative investor** – 25% risky: 25% US large cap ~ **Aggressive investor** – 65% risky: 39% US large cap, 18% US mid-small

cap, 8% international

retirement date

Once you reach your retirement date and start to live off your savings, there are many variables to consider when setting both your risky to not-so-risky ratios and dynamic diversification percentages for your distribution period. They include your health, the health of your spouse, the size of your projected RMD payments, and the amount of your remaining savings.

That's why it's a good idea to reassess your numbers on your rebalancing and reassessing dates. And even though circumstances may change, fill in your distribution years now too, just as you did for your pre-retirement years.

Plan Year ~ Conservative Ratio ~ Aggressive Ratio: Dynamic Diversification

26 ~ **24**-76 ~ **65**-35: **Conservative investor** – 24% risky: 24% US large cap ~ **Aggressive investor** – 65% risky: 39% US large cap, 18% US mid-small cap, 8% international

27 ~ **24**-76 ~ **65**-35: **Conservative investor** – 24% risky: 24% US large cap ~ **Aggressive investor** – 65% risky: 39% US large cap, 18% US mid-small cap, 8% international

28 ~ **23**-77 ~ **64**-36: **Conservative investor** – 23% risky: 23% US large cap ~ **Aggressive investor** – 64% risky: 39% US large cap, 17% US mid-small cap, 8% international

29 ~ **23**-77 ~ **63**-37: **Conservative investor** – 23% risky: 23% US large cap ~ **Aggressive investor** – 63% risky: 39% US large cap, 16% US mid-small cap, 8% international

30 ~ **22**-78 ~ **62**-38: **Conservative investor** – 22% risky: 22% US large cap ~ **Aggressive investor** – 62% risky: 39% US large cap, 15% US mid-small cap, 8% international

31 ~ **21**-79 ~ **61**-39: **Conservative investor** – 21% risky: 21% US large cap ~ **Aggressive investor** – 61% risky: 39% US large cap, 14% US mid-small cap, 8% international

32 ~ **20**-80 ~ **60**-40: **Conservative investor** – 20% risky: 20% US large cap ~ **Aggressive investor** – 60% risky: 39% US large cap, 14% US mid-small cap, 7% international

33 ~ **20**-80 ~ **60**-40: **Conservative investor** – 20% risky: 20% US large cap ~ **Aggressive investor** – 60% risky: 40% US large cap, 14% US mid-small cap, 6% international

34 ~ **20**-80 ~ **60**-40: **Conservative investor** – 20%

risky: 20% US large cap ~ **Aggressive investor** – 60% risky: 41% US large cap, 14% US mid-small cap, 5% international

35 ~ **20**-80 ~ **60**-40: **Conservative investor** – 20% risky: 20% US large cap ~ **Aggressive investor** – 60% risky: 43% US large cap, 13% US mid-small cap, 4% international

36 ~ **20**-80 ~ **60**-40: **Conservative investor** – 20% risky: 20% US large cap ~ **Aggressive investor** – 60% risky: 45% US large cap, 12% US mid-small cap, 3% international

37 ~ **20**-80 ~ **60**-40: **Conservative investor** – 20% risky: 20% US large cap ~ **Aggressive investor** – 60% risky: 46% US large cap, 12% US mid-small cap, 2% international

38 ~ **20**-80 ~ **60**-40: **Conservative investor** – 20% risky: 20% US large cap ~ **Aggressive investor** – 60% risky: 48% US large cap, 11% US mid-small cap, 1% international

39 ~ **20**-80 ~ **60**-40: **Conservative investor** – 20% risky: 20% US large cap ~ **Aggressive investor** – 60% risky: 49% US large cap, 11% US mid-small cap

40 ~ **20**-80 ~ **60**-40: **Conservative investor** – 20% risky: 20% US large cap ~ **Aggressive investor** –

60% risky: 50% US large cap, 10% US mid-small cap

Appendix B: Consolidated Examples (page 217) combines the above, the range of risky to not-so-risky ratios, and the dynamic diversification from both sides of the ratio for all three examples.

Dynamic Diversification-Not-So-Risky Side

Most investments on the not-so-risky side are fixed-income-type investments. Money is loaned for a fixed time at a fixed interest rate. At the end of the loan, known as the maturity date, the amount of the original investment is returned to the lender (you) along with any unpaid interest.

Like risky investments, not-so-risky investments have different degrees of risk too. Fixed-income investments face two types of risk: Business risk and interest rate risk. A fixed-income investment with a large degree of both business and interest rate risk is much riskier and potentially more profitable than one with lesser risk.

You're potentially rewarded for taking extra risks. Instead of dividends and capital gains like on the risky side, on the not-so-risky side it's higher interest payments. That's assuming things go as planned. That's how most corporate bonds, government bonds, and CDs work.

Business Risk

Just as smaller companies offer greater risk on the stock side, it's the same with bonds. The ability of the bond issuer to pay the interest payments as promised through to maturity, as well as returning the principal, is known as business risk.

The higher the business risk the higher the potential return. Smaller corporations, municipalities, and large corporations in trouble have higher default rates than other more stable entities. Thus, they are forced to pay higher interest rates on their bond offerings to attract capital.

You can earn remarkably high rates of return on so-called junk bonds, or in the mutual fund and ETF worlds what are known as high-yield funds, but your default risk is higher.

Being in default means the bond issuer stopped paying the interest per the contract. This usually means that a corporation or municipality is in bankruptcy. What you end up with ultimately lies with the bankruptcy court. The good news is bondholders are closer to the front of the line as far as repayment goes.

Fewer defaults occur when the economy is doing well, and more when it's not. You can minimize that business risk by only loaning money (buying bonds) from big strong financial entities, like the US federal government for example.

The rub is that these safer bonds earn the lowest rate of return. You can manage your business risk and boost your rate of return by buying bonds with varying degrees of business risk.

Interest Rate Risk

Interest rate risk is the chance of interest rates moving higher after you've locked in your fixed rate of return. The longer the maturity period the greater your interest rate risk and the bigger your rate of return.

For example, say you bought a 30-year bond yielding 3 percent, and interest rates subsequently doubled. That means new 30-year bonds are being issued at around 6% with the same risk level as your bond, which means your bond is now worth less on the open market.

Assuming the bond issuer hasn't defaulted, you'll still get your promised 3% return and eventually the return of your principal, but that now represents a below rate of return with which you'll have to suffer. If you (or your fund manager) decided to sell that bond before maturity, less money than the original principal would be

Getting More Involved

received on the sale because of those higher interest rates.

Instead of interest rates going up, let's assume, expounding on the previous example, that interest rates decreased by 50%. Now your bond is worth more, whether you hang on to it and enjoy an above-average rate of return or sell it at a premium.

As you would expect, a bond purchased with a shorter maturity period, say six months, is less affected by the doubling or halving of interest rates, as the holder endures the circumstances for a much shorter period (6 months versus 30 years).

Just as with business risk, the more interest rate risk you take on, the higher your potential rate of return. A diversified portfolio of short, intermediate, and long-term bonds with varying degrees of interest rate risk can positively manage volatility on the not-so-risky side and still earn you a decent return.

Bonds

Bond ownership options include individual bond holdings, bond mutual funds both actively and passively managed, and bond ETFs.

As mentioned, most bonds have a fixed interest

rate that is locked in at the time of issue. That interest payment is what's paid to the bondholder, whether it be monthly, quarterly, yearly, or at maturity.

A bond's market value, however, is not locked in. It varies between its issuance and maturity, going up and down for a variety of reasons, but mostly because of the movement of interest rates. However, that bond's market value eventually returns to what's known as the bond's par value: What the bond was originally sold for when it was issued.

Most bonds are not bought and sold at the original offering price. Bonds are liquid securities that can be sold at market value. Sale prices may vary greatly from the bond's original par value.

Money Market Accounts

The reason money market accounts are considered a "cash" investment and super-safe is that both the interest rate risk and business risk are very low.

Money is lent to only the biggest and strongest financial entities, which reduces business risk. And the lending period is hours or days, not months or years, reducing the amount of time things could go wrong. Things would seriously have to go to hell in a handbasket for those types of loans to default and put your money in danger.

To protect yourself even further, find a money market account that carries FDIC insurance. The Federal Deposit Insurance Corporation, a federal agency created by Congress, insures accounts up to $250,000 per account type, $500,000 if it's a joint account.

Keep in mind that FDIC insurance protects you in case the financial entity who sold you the money market fails. Identity theft, computer piracy, and other forms of fraud are not covered.

There is a huge disparity between the interest rates offered on money markets. Don't settle for less. Only use money markets that pay the highest rates of return.

That's probably not at your local mega-bank branch. Search around. Online banks without brick-and-mortar locations often offer the highest rates. Seek out FDIC insurance, a good reputation, 2-factor authentication, and that higher rate, even if you must give up a bit of convenience. Every little bit helps.

Savings Accounts
Savings accounts offered by banks may offer higher rates than money markets. Like with

money markets, look for FDIC insurance, a good reputation, 2-factor authentication, as well as that high rate.

Certificates of Deposit
CDs are fixed-income investments, much like most bonds. The big difference is a hefty penalty accompanies liquidation of a CD before its maturity date.

Like bonds, CDs have varying maturity lengths, and usually offer higher interest rates the further out the maturity date. They carry the same interest rate risk as bonds, but the business risk can be "eliminated" with FDIC insurance.

Much like money markets and savings accounts, interest rates offered on CDs can vary greatly, so shop around.

Transitioning Dynamically
Just as the risky side of your investment plan gets more conservative as you march towards your goal's fruition, so should your not-so-risky side. As you rebalance and reassess each year, get more conservative with your not-so-risky diversification, favoring investments with less business and interest rate risk.

By the time your goal's fruition date is one year or less, all money in the plan should be invested in the least risky of the least risky. That goes for aggressive investors, conservative investors, and everyone in between. That's what I mean by transitioning dynamically.

Do it on both sides of your risky to not-so-risky ratio. This ensures a fickle stock market doesn't prevent you from achieving your financial goals.

Diversification-Not-So-Risky Side Example #1

Example #1, if you recall, is a short-term goal of 2 years. The risky to not-so-risky ratios and dynamic diversification for an ultra-conservative and super-aggressive portfolio are as follows:

Plan Year ~ Conservative Ratio ~ Aggressive Ratio: Dynamic Diversification

1 ~ 0-**100** ~ 0-**100**: **Conservative investor** – 100% not-so-risky: all in short-term CDs and FDIC-insured high-yield savings/money market accounts ~ **Aggressive investor** – 100% not-so-risky: 50% short-term bond fund, 50% short-term CDs and FDIC-insured high-yield savings/money market accounts

2 ~ 0-**100** ~ 0-**100**: **Conservative investor** – 100% not-so-risky: all in short-term CDs and FDIC-insured high-yield savings/money market accounts ~ **Aggressive investor** – 100% not-so-

risky: all in short-term CDs and FDIC-insured high-yield savings/money market accounts

Conservative investors should stick with short-term CDs, FDIC-insured high-yield saving accounts, and money market accounts for both investing years. Even for more aggressive investors, two years is too short a time to invest in stock.

Diversification-Not-So-Risky Side Example #2

Example #2 is a medium-term educational goal of 10 years (for an 8-year-old) with a 4-year distribution period. The risky to not-so-risky ratios and dynamic diversification for an ultra-conservative and super-aggressive portfolio are as follows:

Plan Year ~ Conservative Ratio ~ Aggressive Ratio: Dynamic Diversification

1 ~ 25-**75** ~ 75-**25**: **Conservative investor** – *75% not-so-risky:* all in total bond market fund ~ **Aggressive investor** – *25% not-so-risky:* all in total bond market fund

2 ~ 23-**77** ~ 70-**30**: **Conservative investor** – *77% not-so-risky:* all in total bond market fund ~ **Aggressive investor** – *30% not-so-risky:* all in total bond market fund

3 ~ 21-**79** ~ 65-**35: Conservative investor** – *79% not-so-risky:* all in total bond market fund ~ **Aggressive investor** – *35% not-so-risky:* all in total bond market fund

4 ~ 18-**82** ~ 60-**40: Conservative investor** – *82% not-so-risky:* all in total bond market fund ~ **Aggressive investor** – *40% not-so-risky:* all in total bond market fund

5 ~ 15-**85** ~ 50-**50: Conservative investor** – *85% not-so-risky:* all in total bond market fund ~ **Aggressive investor** – *50% not-so-risky:* all in total bond market fund

A total bond market fund buys short, intermediate, and longer-term bonds. Dynamic diversification allows even super-conservative investors to own riskier longer-term and business risk-heavy not-so-risky investments when the time horizon allows, as it does here in the first 5 years of example #2.

Plan Year ~ Conservative Ratio ~ Aggressive Ratio

6 ~ 12-**88** ~ 45-**55: Conservative investor** – 88% not-so-risky: 75% total bond market fund, 13% short-term bond fund ~ **Aggressive investor** – 55% not-so-risky: all in total bond market fund

7 ~ 9-**91** ~ 40-**60: Conservative investor** – 91% not-so-risky: 60% total bond market fund, 31% short-term bond fund ~ **Aggressive investor** – 60% not-so-risky: 55% total bond market fund, 5% short-term bond fund

8 ~ 6-**94** ~ 35-**65: Conservative investor** – 94% not-so-risky: 45% total bond market fund, 49% short-term bond fund ~ **Aggressive investor** – 65% not-so-risky: 50% total bond market fund, 15% short-term bond fund

9 ~ 3-**97** ~ 30-**70: Conservative investor** – 97% not-so-risky: 25% total bond market fund, 52% short-term bond fund, 20% mixture of money markets and CDs that carry FDIC insurance ~ **Aggressive investor** – 70% not-so-risky: 40% total bond market fund, 30% short-term bond fund

10 ~ 0-**100** ~ 25-**75: Conservative investor** – 100% not-so-risky: 5% total bond market fund, 45% short-term bond fund, 50% mixture of money markets and CDs that carry FDIC insurance ~

Aggressive investor – 75% not-so-risky: 25% total bond market fund, 30% short-term bond fund, 20% mixture of money markets and CDs that carry FDIC insurance and ultra-short bond funds

off to college

Plan Year ~ Conservative Ratio ~ Aggressive Ratio: Dynamic Diversification

11~ 0-**100** ~ 20-**80: Conservative investor** – *100% not-so-risky: 20% short-term bond fund, 80% mixture of* money markets and CDs that carry FDIC insurance ~ **Aggressive investor** – *80% not-so-risky: 40% short-term bond fund, 40% mixture of* money markets and CDs that carry FDIC insurance and ultra-short bond funds

12 ~ 0-**100** ~ 10-**90: Conservative investor** – *100% not-so-risky: 10% short-term bond fund, 90% mixture of* money markets and CDs that carry FDIC insurance ~ **Aggressive investor** – *90% not-so-risky: 35% short-term bond fund, 55% mixture of* money markets and CDs that carry FDIC insurance

13 ~ 0-**100** ~ 5-**95: Conservative investor** – *100% not-so-risky: mixture of* money markets and CDs that carry FDIC insurance ~ **Aggressive investor** – *95% not-so-risky: 35% short-term bond fund, 65%*

mixture of money markets and CDs that carry FDIC insurance

14 ~ 0-**100** ~ 0-**100: Conservative investor** – *100% not-so-risky: mixture of* money markets and CDs that carry FDIC insurance ~ **Aggressive investor** – *100% not-so-risky: mixture of* money markets and CDs that carry FDIC insurance

As with any financial goal, the closer you are to making withdrawals from your investment plan, the more conservative you want to be with your dynamic diversification. Both ultra-conservative and super-aggressive investors should be 100% invested in the safest of investments in the last year of the plan.

Diversification-Not-So-Risky Side Example #3

You'll remember example #3 is a long-term retirement goal, with withdrawals to start in 25 years. The not-so-risky ratios and dynamic diversification for ultra-conservative and super-aggressive portfolios are as follows:

Plan Year ~ Conservative Ratio ~ Aggressive Ratio: Dynamic Diversification

1 ~ 70-**30** ~ 99-**1: Conservative investor** – 30% not-so-risky: 30% *total bond market fund* ~ **Aggressive investor** – 1% not-so-risky: all in total bond market

fund

2 ~ 68-**32** ~ 99-**1**: **Conservative investor** – 32% not-so-risky: 32% *total bond market fund* ~ **Aggressive investor** – 1% not-so-risky: all in total bond market fund

3 ~ 66-**34** ~ 98-**2**: **Conservative investor** – 34% not-so-risky: 34% *total bond market fund* ~ **Aggressive investor** – 2% not-so-risky: all in total bond market fund

4 ~ 64-**36** ~ 98-**2**: **Conservative investor** – 36% not-so-risky: all in total bond market fund ~ **Aggressive investor** – 2% not-so-risky: all in total bond market fund

5 ~ 62-**38** ~ 96-**4**: **Conservative investor** – 38% not-so-risky: all in total bond market fund ~ **Aggressive investor** – 4% not-so-risky: all in total bond market fund

6 ~ 60-**40** ~ 94-**6**: **Conservative investor** – 40% not-so-risky: all in total bond market fund ~ **Aggressive investor** – 6% not-so-risky: all in total bond market fund

7 ~ 58-**42** ~ 92-**8**: **Conservative investor** – 42% not-so-risky: all in total bond market fund ~ **Aggressive investor** – 8% not-so-risky: all in total bond market fund

8 ~ 56-**44** ~ 90-**10**: **Conservative investor** – 44% not-so-risky: all in total bond market fund ~ **Aggressive investor** – 10% not-so-risky: all in total bond market fund

9 ~ 54-**46** ~ 88-**12**: **Conservative investor** – 46% not-so-risky: all in total bond market fund ~ **Aggressive investor** – 12% not-so-risky: all in total bond market fund

10 ~ 52-**48** ~ 86-**14**: **Conservative investor** – 48% not-so-risky: all in total bond market fund ~ **Aggressive investor** – 14% not-so-risky: all in total bond market fund

11 ~ 50-**50** ~ 84-**16**: **Conservative investor** – 50% not-so-risky: all in total bond market fund ~ **Aggressive investor** – 16% not-so-risky: all in total bond market fund

12 ~ 48-**52** ~ 82-**18**: **Conservative investor** – 52% not-so-risky: all in total bond market fund ~ **Aggressive investor** – 18% not-so-risky: all in total bond market fund

13 ~ 46-**54** ~ 80-**20**: **Conservative investor** – 54% not-so-risky: all in total bond market fund ~ **Aggressive investor** – 20% not-so-risky: all in total bond market fund

14 ~ 44-**56** ~ 79-**21**: **Conservative investor** – 56%

not-so-risky: all in total bond market fund ~
Aggressive investor – 21% not-so-risky: all in total
bond market fund

15 ~ 42-**58** ~ 78-**22**: **Conservative investor** – 58%
not-so-risky: all in total bond market fund ~
Aggressive investor – 22% not-so-risky: all in total
bond market fund

A total bond market fund buys short,
intermediate, and longer-term bonds. Dynamic
diversification allows even super-conservative
investors to own riskier longer-term and business
risk-heavy not-so-risky investments when the time
horizon allows, as it does here in the first 15 years
of example #3.

*Plan Year ~ Conservative Ratio ~ Aggressive Ratio:
Dynamic Diversification*

16 ~ 40-**60** ~ 77-**23**: **Conservative investor** – 60%
not-so-risky: 55% total bond market fund, 5%
short-term bond fund ~ **Aggressive investor** – 23%
not-so-risky: all in total bond market fund

17 ~ 38-**62** ~ 76-**24**: **Conservative investor** – 62%
not-so-risky: 50% total bond market fund, 12%
short-term bond fund ~ **Aggressive investor** – 24%
not-so-risky: all in total bond market fund

18 ~ 36-**64** ~ 75-**25**: **Conservative investor** – 64%

not-so-risky: 45% total bond market fund, 19% short-term bond fund ~ **Aggressive investor** – 25% not-so-risky: all in total bond market fund

19 ~ 34-**66** ~ 74-**26**: **Conservative investor** – 66% not-so-risky: 40% total bond market fund, 26% short-term bond fund ~ **Aggressive investor** – 26% not-so-risky: all in total bond market fund

20 ~ 32-**68** ~ 73-**27**: **Conservative investor** – 68% not-so-risky: 35% total bond market fund, 33% short-term bond fund ~ **Aggressive investor** – 27% not-so-risky: all in total bond market fund

21~ 30-**70** ~ 72-**28**: **Conservative investor** – 70% not-so-risky: 30% total bond market fund, 40% short-term bond fund ~ **Aggressive investor** – 28% not-so-risky: all in total bond market fund

22 ~ 29-**71**~ 70-**30**: **Conservative investor** – 71% not-so-risky: 25% total bond market fund, 46% short-term bond fund ~ **Aggressive investor** – 30% not-so-risky: all in total bond market fund

23 ~ 27-**73** ~ 68-**32**: **Conservative investor** – 73% not-so-risky: 20% total bond market fund, 48% short-term bond fund, 5% *mixture of* money markets and CDs that carry FDIC insurance ~ **Aggressive investor** – 32% not-so-risky: all in total bond market fund

24 ~ 26-**74** ~ 66-**34**: **Conservative investor** – 74% not-so-risky: 15% total bond market fund, 49% short-term bond fund, 10% *mixture of* money markets and CDs that carry FDIC insurance ~ **Aggressive investor** – 34% not-so-risky: all in total bond market fund

25 ~ 25-**75** ~ 65-**35**: **Conservative investor** – 75% not-so-risky: 15% total bond market fund, 45% short term bond fund, 15% *mixture of* money markets and CDs that carry FDIC insurance ~ **Aggressive investor** – 35% not-so-risky: 30% total bond market fund, 5% *mixture of* money markets and CDs that carry FDIC insurance

retirement year

Plan Year ~ Conservative Ratio ~ Aggressive Ratio: Dynamic Diversification

26 ~ 24-**76** ~ 65-**35**: **Conservative investor** – 76% not-so-risky: 14% total bond market fund, 40% short-term bond fund, 22% mixture of money markets and CDs that carry FDIC insurance ~ **Aggressive investor** - 35% not-so-risky: 30% total bond market fund, 5% mixture of money markets and CDs that carry FDIC insurance

27 ~ 24-**76** ~ 65-**35**: **Conservative investor** – 76% not-so-risky: 14% total bond market fund, 40%

short-term bond fund, 22% mixture of money markets and CDs that carry FDIC insurance ~ **Aggressive investor** - 35% not-so-risky: 30% total bond market fund, 5% mixture of money markets and CDs that carry FDIC insurance

28 ~ 23-**77** ~ 64-**36: Conservative investor** – 77% not-so-risky: 12% total bond market fund 40% short-term bond fund, 25% mixture of money markets and CDs that carry FDIC insurance ~ **Aggressive investor** – 36% not-so-risky: 30% total bond market fund, 6% mixture of money markets and CDs that carry FDIC insurance

29 ~ 23-**77** ~ 63-**37: Conservative investor** – 77% not-so-risky: 12% total bond market fund 40% short-term bond fund, 25% mixture of money markets and CDs that carry FDIC insurance ~ **Aggressive investor** – 37% not-so-risky: 30% total bond market fund, 7% mixture of money markets and CDs that carry FDIC insurance

30 ~ 22-**78** ~ 62-**38: Conservative investor** – 78% not-so-risky: 11% total bond market fund, 40% short-term bond fund, 27% mixture of money markets and CDs that carry FDIC insurance ~ **Aggressive investor** - 38% not-so-risky: 30% total bond market fund, 8% mixture of money markets and CDs that carry FDIC insurance

31 ~ 21-**79** ~ 61-**39**: **Conservative investor** – 79% not-so-risky: 10% total bond market fund, 40% short-term bond fund, 29% mixture of money markets and CDs that carry FDIC insurance ~ **Aggressive investor** – 39% not-so-risky: 30% total bond market fund, 9% mixture of money markets and CDs that carry FDIC insurance

Once distributions are underway, more conservative investors continue to gravitate towards less risky investments, ones with minimal business and interest rate risk. This includes FDIC-insured, money markets, and CDs. Aggressive investors may delay that migration some, make a play on the direction interest rates are headed, or pursue other not-so-risky alternatives.

Plan Years ~ Conservative Ratio ~ Aggressive Ratio: Dynamic Diversification

Plan Years 32-40 ~ 20-**80** ~ 60-**40**: **Conservative investor** – 80% not-so-risky: Maintain at least 2 years' worth of living expenses in those FDIC-insured super-safe investments with the rest going to a short-term bond fund ~ **Aggressive investor** – 40% not-so-risky: Maintain at least 2-years' worth of living expenses in those FDIC-insured super-safe investments with the rest spread out between a short-term bond fund and total bond market fund

25-plus years is a long time and things change. It's a good idea to reassess your numbers on your rebalancing and reassessing dates and maintain flexibility as to your situation going forward.

Appendix B: Consolidated Examples (page 217) combines the above, the range of risky to not-so-risky ratios, and the dynamic diversification from both sides of the ratio for all three examples.

Rebalancing and Reassessing

At least once a year, it's necessary to rebalance and reassess. The reason rebalancing is necessary is that however you choose to position your risky to not-so-risky ratio and dynamic diversification mix, it's going to get knocked out of whack.

That's mainly due to the volatile risky side of your plan. Rebalancing once a year resets your risk level back to where you want it.

The Same or Less Risky

Remember my rule from the risky to not-so-risky ratio chapter: Never have a more aggressive investment plan next year than you had the year before. Either keep your risk level the same or, per your investment plan, downgrade your risk.

With an ever-decreasing time horizon for investment, this makes sense. That's why rebalancing and reassessing at least once a year is so important.

If the stock market went up last year, which it does much of the time, your risky to not-so-risky ratio is out of whack. Specifically, a bigger portion of your portfolio is now comprised of riskier investments. You're stock-heavy, in this example. Don't rebalance and your plan is riskier than it was the year before, which shouldn't happen.

Other times, when the stock market is down, you're out of whack but different. You end up selling less-risky investments to buy risky ones during the rebalancing process.

Maybe you've left your investment plan alone and haven't rebalanced in quite some time. More than likely your plan is in dire need of rebalancing.

That goes for super-aggressive investors, the super-conservative, and everyone in between. You need to get back to the risk level you predetermined through your planning.

Once you're into your distribution period, don't think you can stop rebalancing and reassessing every year. Now that you're taking distributions, it's more important than ever. Distributions should always come from your least risky bucket:

Those FDIC-insured savings accounts, money markets, and short-term CDs.

That leaves a big hole on your not-so-risky side that needs to be refilled. Rebalancing resets your risk by liquidating risky investments to fill those safe accounts back up to your predetermined risky to not-so-risky ratio and dynamic diversification percentages.

You've created a dynamic investment plan, one that changes from a more aggressive plan to one that's more conservative. That's another one of your duties on your rebalancing and reassessing date: Check your plan to see if it's time for a downshift in risk via your risky to not-so-risky ratio and dynamic diversification.

Resetting Your Risk

You could rebalance twice a year, or even more often if you really want to. Many professional managers do it quarterly or monthly.

I question the utility of that extra effort. If your investment plans contain mostly funds (mutual funds and ETFs), I think once a year is sufficient. Any more is much like "spinning your wheels," and there can be value in keeping your investment plans as simple as possible.

These rebalancing moves shouldn't cost you anything, not even a penny in fees. That's another reason you want to invest with investment companies that have a no load and no brokerage charge trading policy.

Pick a Rebalance and Reassess Date

Don't make this any harder than it has to be. Pick a date and rebalance and reassess on that date every year no matter what. Pick a time of the year that's convenient and easy to remember. This is necessary because I've found of the three risk management strategies, this is often the one that doesn't get done.

If you make a yearly contribution to your investment plan, as many who lack a retirement plan at work or who are self-employed do, that's a good time to rebalance. By allocating that extra money and rebalancing together, you're killing two birds with one stone, as the archaic saying goes. I prefer calling it a twofer. I love time-saving twofers.

Or you could rebalance at tax time. As soon you're done with your taxes for the preceding year, while you still have your accountant hat on, go ahead and rebalance and reassess.

Or you may want to do it during your employer's

open enrollment period, the night of the Summer Solstice, or on International Talk Like a Pirate Day (September 19th). *Arrr. Time to rebalance and reassess, Matey!*

Here's how you do it. Pull out your investment plan. See what your risky to not-so-risky ratio and dynamic diversification are for the next year. It should be either the same or slightly more conservative than the previous year.

If it's the same as last year, simply multiply the new amount of money in your plan by the same diversity percentages you used last year. Shuffle things around so your allocations match the percentages.

If your plan calls for a downshift in risk, multiply that new balance by those new diversity percentages, and shuffle as necessary. The whole process may take up to a week: Often you need to wait a few days after liquidating an investment before the money becomes available to re-invest in another.

With mutual funds, money is often available the next business day after a trade. ETFs and individual shares take longer to settle, usually in a couple of business days. After that last rebalancing transaction, you're done for another year.

Rebalancing and Reassessing Example #1

The risky to not-so-risky ratios for an ultra-conservative and super-aggressive portfolio for a 2-year goal was as follows:

Plan Year ~ Conservative Ratio ~ Aggressive Ratio

1 ~ 0-100 ~ 0-100

2 ~ 0-100 ~ 0-100

Is rebalancing necessary for a short-term goal like Example #1? Yes, especially for aggressive investors. More conservative investors' dynamic diversification will already be invested in those least risky investments by year 2. In that case, no rebalancing would be necessary. Otherwise, that final migration to 100% FDIC-insured accounts needs to be made on that final rebalancing and reassessing date, before the start of plan year 2 in this example.

Rebalancing and Reassessing Example #2

Example #2, if you recall, was for an intermediate-term educational goal of 10 years with a 4-year distribution period. Pretend you're a super-aggressive investor, you're entering plan year 5, and it's your rebalancing and reassessing date. One year ago, you started plan year 4 with $40,000 and the following allocations per the previous example #2s in the risky to not-so-risky and dynamic diversification sections:

Plan Year ~ Aggressive Ratio

4 ~ 60-40

5 ~ 50-50

Plan Year 4: $40,000

30% US large cap fund - $12,000

23% US mid-small cap fund - $9,200

7% total international fund - $2,800

40% total bond market fund - $16,000

In this example, let's pretend you had a great investing year, and your balance jumped $10,000 from plan year 4 to 5, leaving you a balance of $50,000. Plugging in the numbers from example #2 in the previous risk management strategies chapters, you'll need to shuffle your money around a bit to reflect the following:

Plan Year 5: $50,000

30% US large cap fund – $15,000

18% US mid-small cap fund – $9,000

2% international fund – $1,000

50% total bond market fund - $25,000

Looking at your allocations before rebalancing, you'll find them severely out of whack. Specifically, the selling of stock and buying of bonds will be necessary. Not only are you reducing your risky holdings by 10% from plan year 4, but accounting for the risky side's sharp upturn during the previous year.

After a few days of rebalancing, sans any tinkering, you're done rebalancing and reassessing for another year.

Rebalancing and Reassessing Example #3

Example #3 is a long-term retirement goal with withdrawals to begin in 25 years. Pretend you're an ultra-conservative investor, you're about to enter plan year 10, and it's your rebalancing and reassessing date. One year ago, you started plan year 9 with $100,000 and the following allocations per the plan:

Plan Year ~ Conservative Ratio

9 ~ 54-46

10 ~ 52-44

Plan Year 9: $100,000

40% US large-cap stock fund - $40,000

10% US mid-small cap stock fund - $10,000

4% total international stock fund - $4,000

46% total bond market fund - $46,000

In this example, let's pretend you had a horrific investing year, and your retirement plan balance plunged $10,000 to $90,000. Plugging in the numbers from example #3 in the previous risk management strategies chapters, you'll need to shuffle your money around a bit to reflect the following:

Plan Year 10: $90,000

40% US large-cap stock fund - $36,000

10% US mid-small cap stock fund - $9,000

2% total international stock fund - $1,800

48% total bond market fund - $43,200

Looking at your allocations before rebalancing, you'd find them out of whack some. Not only are you changing your allocations slightly from last year, but accounting for the individual volatility of your diversity during the previous year, which was mostly negative on the risky side. That means having to liquidate bonds to buy more stock.

After a few days of rebalancing, sans any tinkering, you're done rebalancing and reassessing for another year.

Modern Portfolio Theory

Modern Portfolio Theory (MPT) was first published by Harry Markowitz in the 1950s. The original hypotheses proposed have held up very well over the years, given historical returns.

The Cliff Notes Version

In a nutshell, MPT is a math-based theory that assembles "efficient" portfolios, given an investor's risk level and expected return:

- **Risk Level** - Defined by the volatility of the investments being considered

- **Expected Return** – Given a particular risk level, the return an investor can anticipate on an investment

Assembled portfolios of diversified investments behave differently than individual securities or lesser diversified portfolios. By diversifying, *unsystematic risk* can be greatly reduced.

You don't need to master MPT to succeed as a stock investor. Suffice it to say most professional money managers use MPT in one form or another, and my stock investing strategies lean heavily on it because it works.

R Squared

"R" a.k.a. the coefficient of determination measures how closely a fund's holdings correlate with an index. R is also a part of complex equations used to calculate both *alpha* and *beta*, two other helpful metrics you can use when evaluating potential investments.

When searching for passively managed funds, look for funds with an r squared closest to 1 (or 100%). 1 or 100% represents an exact correlation with the index. The whole idea behind a true index fund is to replicate the index exactly. Anything less indicates active management, shoddy management, or a poor product.

Follow the index and robot rather than the human? In many areas of your dynamic diversification, yes, that's what I'm saying. Let your research guide you.

When evaluating actively managed investments, seek out the benchmark with the r squared closest to 100% for comparison. Even though it won't be as close to 100% as an index fund, it's still the best way to evaluate that fund's performance, assuming its r squared is greater than 75%.

As warned previously, often Wall Street will compare a lessor-correlated index with an actively managed fund's performance rather than the true benchmark. Don't be fooled. Root out the best-fit index by using r squared.

What if there are no benchmarks available with an r squared greater than 75%? Another measure of volatility, *standard deviation*, can be used instead.

Beta

Beta represents a complex formula that measures how risky an investment is versus its benchmark index. The number one represents a similar risk. Any number less than one indicates less risk than the benchmark, and more than one indicates more risk than the benchmark.

When researching several investments with similar historical returns, favor the one with the lower beta. That investment achieved the same return with less risk, as measured by its volatility. The stock with the lower beta is more apt to outperform the more volatile investment going forward.

Beta (and alpha) should not be used as evaluation tools if an investment's r squared is 75% or less, as r is a component of both formulas.

Alpha

Alpha is yet another formula that measures an investment's performance using several variables. It measures any "excess" an active money manager brought to the table, as measured against a benchmark.

When perusing actively managed funds, one looks for positive alphas. A negative alpha connotates a below benchmark performance, and a positive one a performance above.

Standard Deviation

Unlike beta, standard deviation can't be used as a standalone measurement of volatility. Since standard deviation measures an investment's own volatility with no comparison, the resulting number is pretty much meaningless.

That's why beta is often favored over standard deviation as a volatility barometer, assuming there is a reliable benchmark index. It doesn't require comparisons to be a valid indicator.

Only when an investment's standard deviation is compared to a like investment's standard deviation does the number have any meaning.

Like with beta, given two like investments with similar historical returns, the one with the lower standard deviation should be favored. This indicates less historic volatility and a better chance at future success.

Bogleheads

Mr. Markowitz's theories assumed a zero cost of investment and adequate diversification in a portfolio. Back in the twentieth century when his theories were first proposed, that was difficult if not impossible for an individual investor to achieve.

That is, until another investing pioneer, Jack Bogle came along. He created an investment vehicle that allows investors like you and me to achieve the levels of diversity embraced by MPT and do it at a very low cost.

Mr. Bogle championed his invention, the index mutual fund, as well as his investing philosophies at Vanguard®.

Index funds took a while to catch on, but eventually, they did, at least with a small segment of investors. Not wanting to be outdone, the brokerage industry came up with what in some instances is a better version of an index fund called an exchange-traded fund.

You can embrace the investment philosophies of

the late Mr. Bogle and his "followers" at *Bogleheads.org*.

Passive management has gained in popularity but overall, actively managed assets still outnumber those managed passively. A large part of Wall Street continues to rail on passive management, insisting active management is the only way.

They're correct, of course. Active management is the only way they can make more money off you.

One Plan for Multiple Accounts

Whenever you're using multiple accounts to reach a single financial goal, you don't want multiple investment plans. Treat them all as one. This makes your investment plan much easier to manage.

As an example, during our active earning years, my wife Katherine and I at one time were investing in six different tax-advantaged accounts, plus a regular taxable one, all for the same goal of financial independence. You may have even more:

1. 401(k)-Keith

2. Roth IRA-Kat

3. Roth IRA-Keith

4. Traditional IRA-Kat

5. Traditional IRA-Keith

6. Health Savings Account-Keith

7. Regular Taxable Account-Joint

Instead of seven different investment plans for each account, figure out how to combine them into one single account, figuratively speaking. This can be accomplished with a customized Excel® spreadsheet, your broker's software, or an investing app.

That means one of your tax-advantaged accounts may contain mostly interest-generating bonds. Another could be heavy on actively managed mutual funds and dividend-paying stocks, while your regular taxable account could contain mostly growth EFTs.

Looking individually at each account, the investments appear random and inappropriate. Looking at all the investments aggregately, however, and you should see a perfectly balanced portfolio inoculated with my three risk management strategies, just the right amount of risk, and optimized to save on taxes.

Don't just divide up your investment plan

arbitrarily. Learn more about your home country's tax code and strategically position your dynamic diversification where it will have the biggest bang for the buck from a tax standpoint. This gives you yet another opportunity to save money and increase your after-tax rate of return.

How Ordinary Income is Taxed

In the United States, ordinary income includes wages, salaries, tips, bonuses, commissions, rents, and royalties. As far as your investments go, interest income, non-qualified dividends, short-term capital gains, and stock awards are also taxed as ordinary income.

Currently, ordinary income tax rates are graduated and range from 10% to 37%. The more ordinary income you have, the higher your effective tax rate.

Of all the taxes, ordinary income tax rates are the highest for most taxpayers. That's why you want to minimize the effect of those higher rates by delaying or eliminating that type of tax in your investment plan.

How Interest is Taxed

Interest is taxed as ordinary income. Keep investments that generate lots of interest out of regular taxable accounts since ordinary income rates are the highest. Better to have the tax on that interest delayed (traditional) or eliminated (Roth).

Interest is mostly earned by the not-so-risky side of your investment plan. That's where you'll find bonds, CDs, high-yield savings accounts, and money markets, all of which generate interest income.

How Non-Qualified Dividends are Taxed

Non-qualified dividends, which are sure to be generated by your investment plan, are lumped together with the above and taxed as ordinary income too.

International investments that don't meet IRS guidelines for a lower capital gains rate are frequent culprits, as are domestic REITs. Try and keep these types of investments out of your regular taxable account too.

How Qualified Dividends are Taxed

Qualified dividends, which do meet IRS guidelines, are taxed at a lower 15% rate. Because of that low rate, it's less painful having investments that generate qualified dividends, like US value stocks, in your regular taxable account.

If you're planning to become financially independent before age 59 1/2, living off your qualified dividend income generated by investments in your regular taxable account is one of the tax-savvy ways to do it.

How Capital Gains are Taxed

Short-term capital gains, which are gains generated from the sale of stock with less than a one year holding period, are taxed at that higher ordinary income tax rate. Like other ordinary income-generating investments, try and keep short-term capital gains to a minimum in your regular taxable account.

Long-term capital gains, on the other hand, are taxed at that low 15% rate. 15% is probably less than your effective ordinary income tax rate, so keeping investments that generate them in your regular taxable account isn't so bad either.

Deferring Income with Growth ETFs

Still, even though long-term capital gains are not taxed at higher rates, it's still taxed, and might negatively affect your tax situation in other ways too. That's why I favor individual growth stocks and growth ETFs in regular taxable accounts when possible.

Growth stocks pay lower dividend rates than value stocks, and if you're holding individual growth shares, there are no capital gains unless you decide to generate them. That's the problem with growth mutual funds, especially actively managed ones. You need to pay tax on both short- and long-term capital gains realized by the fund every year, even if you didn't liquidate any shares.

Positioning growth EFTs in your regular taxable account is a good solution. Dividends are kept to a minimum versus value stocks, and a good growth ETF manager can delay most or all capital gains until you sell shares. Again, that's unlike growth mutual funds, where capital gains tax liability passes through to shareholders every year.

Find Your Perfect Mix

What your mix of accounts looks like will depend on the size of your portfolio and the ratio of your tax-advantaged to regular taxable account holdings. Of course, many stock investors save for retirement exclusively in tax-advantaged accounts and don't even own a regular taxable brokerage account.

Whether you put interest-generating investments in a Roth or traditional account has a lot to do with where you're at. If you've got double-digit years left before the start of your distribution period, I prefer putting interest-generating investments in traditional accounts over Roth accounts since these are your lower-yielding investments.

When a longer time horizon warrants their inclusion, reserve Roth investments for your triples and home runs, to use my previous analogy. Since you expect those investments to have the biggest gains, ensuring those gains will be 100% tax-free is another way to boost your after-tax rate of return.

If you're further along and are close to or are already taking distributions, risky investments have become a lesser part of the mix. That means more and more interest-bearing investments in your Roth as your investment plan progresses.

Maybe You Need 2 Plans?

If you have more than ample resources for retirement and love your beneficiaries, you may want to consider constructing two investment plans for retirement: One for your regular taxable account and traditional assets, the other for all or a portion of your Roth assets.

The idea is to split up your assets into two separate investment plans, each with its own time horizon. Your first plan is the one you're going to live on in retirement, given an average lifespan. End that time horizon on the date you anticipate starting withdrawals from the first plan.

Fund the first plan with any regular taxable accounts and traditional assets as needed. If you've been saving mostly in Roth accounts, include Roth money as necessary in that first plan too.

The end of an average lifespan, by the way, coincides with the last payments from your traditional accounts because of required minimum distributions. Based on retirees turning age 73 in 2025, those last RMD payments come when you're in your mid-eighties, assuming life expectancies remain the same and you're lucky enough to live that long.

The projected date of that last RMD payment from your traditional reserves will serve as the end of your time horizon for your second investment plan. Assuming you retired in 2025, that would be somewhere around the year 2038.

If you've been paying attention, a longer time horizon should ensure a higher rate of return no matter your risk tolerance. In my example, the second plan would start with a time horizon that is 13 years longer than the first investment plan. If you live an average lifespan, that means a bigger probate-free and tax-free inheritance for your loved ones from your Roth holdings.

Or, if you live longer than average, you'll have plenty of tax-free money to live out your life. That is, assuming things don't go to hell in a handbasket.

By creating that second investment plan and saving your Roth IRA till last, you've created both a powerful wealth-building tool as well as a simple way to pass along money to your loved ones. It's a win-win for all. Just make sure to properly fill out your Roth IRA beneficiary statement, and keep it updated.

Tax-Advantaged Accounts

Investing in tax-advantaged accounts is like getting a big head start in a foot race. You're not guaranteed to win the race, but the chances you'll succeed are greatly enhanced.

Many shun tax-advantaged accounts because they have restrictions. One reason I favor them is because of those restrictions. Most bar you from tapping the money in the account without penalty until later, which is a good thing. Those restrictions force you into investing for the longer term, allowing the power of compounding to work its magic.

There's also a lot less paperwork to do in a tax-advantaged account when compared to a regular taxable account come tax time. There's no need to keep track of the basis of your contributions nor your reinvested dividends, capital gains, and interest when investing in a tax-advantaged account.

Directing money to tax-advantaged accounts is yet another way you can stack the deck in your favor. There are many available, and some have features and advantages which you may not be aware of.

401(k)-Type Plans

If you have a retirement plan at work, it's more than likely in the form of a 401(k), 401(a), 403(b), 457, TSP, or other employer-offered defined contribution plans. I call these plans 401(k)-type plans because although they differ most of the important attributes affecting employees are the same.

Other retirement plans don't come close to the amount of tax-advantaged money per year you can contribute. That's why I recommend looking at your employer's plan first when searching for your best tax-advantaged plan. Being able to contribute to a good 401(k)-type plan is a potential game-changer.

High Contribution Limits

You can contribute over three times as much to 401(k)-type plans as you can to IRAs. Depending on your level of income, you may be able to contribute to both, boosting your advantages even more.

401(k) Max Contribution Age 49 and Younger 2025	
Regular Contribution	**$23,500**

If you're age 50 or older, you get to add on the catch-up contribution (or the enhanced catch-up if you're ages 60-63), increasing your maximum even more:

401(k) Max Contributions Age 50 and Older 2025	
Regular Contribution	+$23,500
Catch-Up Contribution	+$7,500
	=$31,000

401(k) Max Contributions Ages 60-63 for 2025	
Regular Contribution	+$23,500
Enhanced Catch-Up Contribution	+$11,250
	=$34,750

Starting in 2025, there is an enhanced catch-up limit for savers ages 60-63. By rule, the yearly limit is the greater of $10,000 or 150% of the year's regular catch-up.

Employee catch-up contributions are limited to Roth-only designated contributions past the wage threshold of $145,000 for 2025.

If you're just getting started, those lofty yearly

maximums may seem -more than enough. Still, if you're behind in your retirement savings or striving for financial independence, you need to act on every advantage available.

Matching Money

If your employer offers a match, that's a wonderful thing. *You want to do everything in your power to receive the full match every year.* It's free money, right?

It's not free. It's a part of your compensation package. That's how both your employer and Uncle Sam look at it, and so should you. If you want to work for free, contribute less than the full match.

Your match is always made as a pre-tax or traditional contribution. Even if you make all Roth contributions, your match will be deposited into your account pre-tax.

Some employers require you to make contributions in all pay periods throughout the year to get the full match. Other more enlightened employers offer no such restrictions: You're guaranteed your full match via a *true-up* feature no matter when you make the required contributions. Check the details of your employer's plan to be certain.

Who's Your Employer's Custodian?

Every employer who starts a 401(k)-type plan must choose a financial institution to host it. These "custodians," as they are called, are chosen from the hundreds of investment companies that offer these services. For example, your employer might have chosen Fidelity® Investments as their custodian.

You sign into your account through the custodian's portal, and most if not all your investment options are from their lineup. Bigger companies and enlightened smaller ones may have offerings from multiple investment firms, and access to a brokerage link where you can invest outside of your employer's options.

Most employers who offer plans, I've found, do a decent job with their offerings. Still, make no mistake, some 401(k)-type plans are better than others. When looking for a job, don't forget to check out the retirement plans offered, along with everything else.

Because of regulations, a 401(k)-type plan can be complicated and expensive to open and operate, especially for smaller businesses. Watch out for employers who may have compromised the quality of investment options in exchange for lower start-up fees.

Whether employers choose these over-charging custodians out of ignorance or tight cash flow, most probably don't realize the harm they're doing to both their employees and themselves. Since most employers save for their retirement using the same plan, they're limiting their own wealth-building too. It doesn't take long for high investment fees to dwarf any initial upfront savings.

If you have a dog plan (*https://keithdorney.com/dog-plan*), as I like to call them, you have my sympathies. Luckily, there are plenty of alternatives.

With most 401(k)-type plans, the expense ratios of the offered funds should be your only cost of investment. If there are additional fees, that's not a good sign: That's a characteristic of a dog plan.

For example, there may be brokerage fees or loads for changing investments, yearly account fees, redemption fees, and ridiculous fees like the dreaded 12b-1.

Beware of High Expense Ratios

Just because your 401(k)-type plan doesn't have those extra fees, doesn't mean you're out of the woods yet. Check the various expense ratios of the offered funds. Are those ratios closer to .05% or

.5%?

Keep in mind that the difference in investment expenses repeats year after year. With your increasing balance, the fees just keep getting bigger and bigger. Do the math, and over the years we're talking about tens of thousands of dollars in lost investments.

Reaching Age 59 1/2

If you're age 59 1/2 or older and have a dog plan, there is a workaround. Reaching that magic age not only gives you the ability to withdraw money penalty-free but to do what is known as an *in-service withdrawal*. Once a year, you're able to roll over the balance of your dog plan to a traditional and/or Roth IRA of your choosing without any tax or penalty.

Make the maximum contribution you can afford to your dog plan even though you'll have to suffer through the year with those high fees. Then roll over every penny to IRAs at a custodian of your choosing.

You're still stuck with those high fees, but only until the next year comes around when you can roll your money out of there once again. This strategy lets you take advantage of those high 401k-type plan contribution limits in those crucial last years before retiring as well as minimizing your stock investing expense.

After leaving your employer for another job or retiring, your money stays with your former employer's custodian unless you act. If you do nothing, you'd still have access to your custodian's portal for management purposes, but no new contributions are allowed.

Your other options are rolling that money tax and penalty-free to the 401(k)-type plan set up at your next employer's custodian or rolling it tax and penalty-free to a traditional IRA (and a Roth IRA if you made Roth contributions).

After-Tax Contributions

Some 401(k) type plans, besides traditional and Roth contributions, allow a third type of contribution called an *after-tax contribution*. This allows you to contribute more, in some cases much more, to your 401(k)-type plan than the annual contribution limit.

Don't even think about making an after-tax contribution, however, unless you've already planned to max out your regular contributions (pre-tax and/or Roth). That's because tax-wise the after-tax contribution is inferior to both a Roth and traditional contribution, and it won't qualify for any company match.

The limit for after-tax contributions varies per your company plan. Some employers have a set dollar limit for after-tax contributions. Others don't, but you're still limited by federal law governing 401(k)-type plans, which have a maximum contribution limit in addition to the yearly "regular" contribution limit.

If your plan has no set after-tax contribution maximum, compute your maximum after-tax contribution amount by subtracting your pre-tax, Roth, and any company match contributions from the appropriate allowable maximums.

After-Tax Contribution Example

Sara, a higher wage earner, is age 38 and wants to make the maximum contribution to her 401(k)-type plan. Her company offers a generous $15,000 match on the maximum contribution with no set limit on after-tax contributions. How much can she contribute, using the maximums from the 2025 tax year?

401(k) Max *All* Contributions Age 49 and Younger for 2025	
Regular Contribution	+$23,500
Company Match	+$15,000
After-Tax Contribution	+$31,500
Total Allowed	**=$70,000**

So how much can Sara contribute? That's around three times more than the 401(k) regular contribution and more than ten times the IRA contribution limits.

Folks age 50 and older at Sara's company can contribute even more:

401(k) Max *All* Contributions Age 50 and Older for 2025	
Regular Contribution	+$23,500
Company Match	+$15,000
Catch-Up Contribution	+$7,500
After-Tax Contribution	+$31,500
Total	**=$77,500**

401(k) Max *All* Contributions Ages 60-63 for 2025	
Regular Contribution	+$23,500
Company Match	+$15,000
Enhanced Catch-Up Contribution	+$11,250
After-Tax Contribution	+$31,500
Total	**=$81,250**

Plus, if her plan allows, she can execute a mega back door Roth and further her advantage even more.

Those high contribution limits might seem like more than enough per year, especially if you're on the younger side and dedicating parts of your most important money to financial goals other than retirement. Once again, if you're striving to become financially independent, want to retire early, or you're approaching retirement and are a little behind, those high maximums are a godsend.

Mega Backdoor Roth Conversion

If your employer's 401(k)-type plan doesn't offer after-tax contributions, it's best to skip this next part. It will only make you jealous.

Some enlightened employers not only offer an after-tax contribution as part of their plan but the ability to either recharacterize or convert those contributions to Roth. If this transformation is done immediately once the after-tax contribution is made, no earnings will be generated on the contribution, and the conversion will be tax-free.

By law, accumulated associated earnings from after-tax contributions must be converted along with the contribution. Those earnings are taxable in the year the contribution was made. Immediate recharacterization or conversion of after-tax contributions prevents any earnings from occurring.

Set your after-tax payroll deduction percentage for the year so it generates the amount you want to contribute after-tax. This is in addition to setting a contribution percentage for your regular contributions. Further, check to see if your plan facilitates immediate recharacterization or conversion and set it up so it's done automatically.

Once recharacterized or converted, earnings now accrue tax-free rather than tax-deferred, which of course is way better.

Most Roth conversions result in more tax liability for the year for the converter. Not so with what has become known as a *mega-backdoor Roth*. If done right, there shouldn't be any extra tax liability.

For the record, I coined this maneuver The "'Ole Roth Switcheroo" over a decade ago, but the name never caught on. There are two types of *switcheroos*:

401(k)-Type Plan Switcheroo

If your employer's plan allows it, you can immediately recharacterize your after-tax contribution to Roth. With this option, your after-tax contribution never leaves your 401(k)-type plan. After the conversion, that after-tax contribution has the same status as any regular Roth contributions you might have made: They can't be withdrawn penalty-free until age 59 1/2.

Roth IRA Switcheroo

Your other option is to convert those after-tax contributions to a Roth IRA. This option is best if you want to use some or all those after-tax conversions for a shorter-term financial goal.

5 years after the conversion, the amount you converted can be withdrawn tax and penalty-free from your Roth IRA. You don't have to be age 59 1/2 or have a good reason. Each year's conversions have their own 5-year window.

These conversions are allowed for employees even if they're over the AGI limits for making a direct Roth contribution. In my after-tax contribution example, my lucky higher-wage-earning employee Sara was able to fund her Roth IRA with more than four times what is allowed by the Roth IRA contribution limits. This is despite the fact she's prohibited from making a direct Roth IRA contribution because she's over the Roth IRA income limits (page 181).

But is it Legal?

If this sounds sneaky and underhanded to you, you're not alone. Let me indulge you in a brief history of how these peculiar strategies came into being. It may make you a little more comfortable executing them.

Back in 2010, the IRS rescinded the previously-in-place AGI limits for Roth conversions. I believe Uncle Sam figured he was losing out on tons of immediate tax revenue by not allowing wealthier taxpayers to convert pre-tax money to Roth.

What I'm sure they didn't anticipate was opening the mega back door portal, giving a tremendous advantage to a select number of taxpayers who have this option in their 401(k)-type plan.

Since 2010, I've taught thousands of employees these strategies. Many of them were able to reach financial independence quickly, in ten years or less.

For the tax year 2025, Uncle Sam still allows this strategy. Bills proposing eliminating this loophole have been introduced in Congress more than several times, but none of them made it through. If you're one of the lucky ones who are offered this option, exploit this loophole while you still can!

Self-Employment Options

If you're self-employed, you've got lots of choices for plans with high contribution limits. Since you're setting the plan up yourself, you can be sure to choose a custodian who offers great investment options and low fees.

Depending on your circumstances, a SEP-IRA, SIMPLE IRA/401(k), Keogh, or Solo 401(k) could fit the bill nicely. Meet with a financial advisor fiduciary to discuss a retirement plan for your small business if you don't have one already. Even if the business is just you, there are lots of high-contribution options that are relatively easy and inexpensive to set up.

Roth IRA

If you don't already have a Roth IRA, you should open one up and fund it up to the maximum allowed for the tax year:

IRA Max Contribution Age 49 and Younger 2025	
Regular Contribution	**$7,000**

IRA Max Contributions Age 50 and Older 2025	
Regular Contribution	+$7,000
Catch-Up Contribution	+$1,000
	=$8,000

Whether you're making all Roth contributions or all traditional contributions, or you're making both Roth and traditional contributions, your combined contributions for the year cannot exceed these thresholds.

A Roth IRA also has income restrictions. If you make too much, your ability to contribute directly to a Roth IRA could be limited:

Roth IRA Income Limits 2025			
Filing Method	Max Allowed	Partial Allowed	None Allowed
Single, Married Filing Separately, Head of Household	**MAGI less than $150,000**	**MAGI 150,000 - $165,000**	**MAGI greater than $165,000**
Married Filing Jointly	**MAGI less than $236,000**	**MAGI $236,000 - $246,000**	**MAGI greater than $246,000**

If your employer doesn't offer a plan or they do and the plan doesn't offer a Roth option, you really need a Roth IRA. Even if your employer offers a Roth option and you're making all Roth contributions, you still need a Roth IRA for several important reasons.

Accessibility

Few accounts offer the ability to tap funds before age 59 1/2 without tax or penalty. Roth IRAs are the exception. Your principal contributions over the years are assessable for any reason without tax or penalty.

You don't have to be of a certain age, nor have a good reason for the withdrawal. I've found a lot of people aren't aware of that, which in many cases is just as well.

Keep in mind the earnings generated by your Roth IRA principal contributions cannot be withdrawn tax and penalty-free until you reach age 59 1/2, so be sure and leave that part alone. In fact, try and leave all of it alone so you earn more tax-free interest, dividends, and capital gains. Even if you don't touch it, it's nice to know you have that ability in your back pocket if you need it.

Avoiding RMDs

If you've made or are planning to make Roth contributions to your 401(k)-type plan, you no longer need to roll over those funds into a Roth IRA before your RMD age. Thanks to the Secure 2.0 legislation, Roth contributions and associated earnings left in your employer's plan are no longer subject to Required Minimum Distributions like they were before 2023.

Backdoor Roth Conversion

Even if you're over the Roth IRA income limits for making a direct Roth IRA contribution, you still might be able to contribute to one, but it takes a few extra steps. I coined this maneuver the 'Ole

Roth IRA Switcheroo decades ago, but the name never caught on. It's more widely known today as a *backdoor Roth conversion* from a traditional IRA.

Like the mega back door Roth conversion previously described what you're about to hear sounds a little sneaky and underhanded. However, it's currently all legal and cool with your Uncle Sam.

If you're over the AGI limits for making a Roth contribution, you're way over the limits for making a deductible contribution to a traditional IRA (assuming you have an employer's retirement plan at work). However, anyone can make what's known as a nondeductible contribution to a traditional IRA.

A nondeductible contribution kept in a traditional IRA earns tax-deferred income, not tax-free like in a Roth IRA. As the name implies, there's no tax deduction on the contribution either. Tax-wise, it's like making an after-tax contribution to your employer's 401(k)-type plan (if they offer that option).

That's why immediately after you make your nondeductible traditional IRA contribution, you convert those funds to a Roth IRA. If you don't have other pre-tax funds in your IRA(s) and no earnings have accumulated on your principal between the contribution and the conversion, the switcheroo will not only be penalty-free but tax-free too. *Now all your future earnings will accumulate tax-free instead of tax deferred.*

Unlike direct contributions to your Roth IRA, which are accessible at any time for any reason with no tax or penalty, converted money won't be accessible tax and penalty-free until five years have passed since the conversion. Keep in mind each year's worth of conversions has its own five-year window.

Like with direct contributions, all future earnings (interest, dividends, and capital appreciation) realized from the converted principal must be left alone until at least age 59 1/2 to be tax and penalty-free upon distribution.

IRS Pro-Rata Rule

If you have other pre-tax contributions and associated earnings in your traditional IRA(s), whether from prior contributions or rollovers, a backdoor Roth conversion probably won't make sense. This is due to the IRS's pro-rata rule, which states you can't just cherry-pick what funds you wish to convert from your traditional IRA. It forces you to convert a "pro-rata" portion of all deductible and nondeductible contributions and associated earnings in your traditional IRA. That means a good hunk of your conversion could be taxable.

Assume you've got $95,000 in your traditional IRA from a previous employer's 401(k) rollover. You decide to execute the switcheroo with a $5,000 nondeductible contribution to your traditional IRA, which you immediately convert to a Roth IRA. Applying the pro-rata rule, 95% of the conversion will be taxed at your ordinary income rate.

If you're a higher wage earner, over the AGI limits for making direct Roth contributions, and not subject to the pro-rata rule, you can fund your Roth IRA every year in this manner up the IRA contribution limit. Once again, what sounds like a sneaky and underhanded maneuver is all perfectly legal, at least for now.

Changes to the tax rules that affect tax-advantaged accounts are the kind of thing I write about in my free monthly *Best Money Newsletter*. Sign up at *https://keithdorney.com/newsletter-sign-up/* and stay informed as to any future changes in those switcheroo rules.

Roth Distributions

When you've got a large swath of tax-free money

in your retirement savings, it opens myriad possibilities:

- Draw on it early on in retirement to keep your taxable income low, which in turn lowers other expenses in retirement like Medicare costs and taxes.

- Save it for the latter years of your retirement. Since you're investing for a longer time, more tax-free earnings pile up, ensuring you don't run out of money. Plus, don't forget about RMDs. Your pre-tax contributions and earnings are subject to RMDs. You'll be forced to start to withdraw those funds whether you want to or not come your mid-seventies.

- Once you've contributed/converted a solid five figures to your Roth IRA(s), consider reducing your emergency reserve fund by half and applying that extra money to your most important financial goal. Over the years, I've noticed I've tapped my emergency reserve fund plenty of times, but rarely did I need all of it. Since principal contributions and eventually conversions to a Roth IRA are assessable anytime for any reason without tax or penalty, use that money as your emergency *emergency* reserve and hope you never have to use it. This strategy can help accelerate the attainment of a particularly important financial goal other than retirement.

Estate Planning Tool

A Roth IRA can be a great estate planning tool. Passing along tax-free cash to the next generation is easily done through a properly filled-out beneficiary statement.

If you've done a good job saving over the years and have a ton of pre-tax contributions and earnings in your retirement accounts, it makes a lot of sense to save that Roth money for later. Besides RMDs, if you're lucky to live longer than average, that tax-free cash will be there for you.

If you don't spend it all, know your beneficiaries will appreciate their tax-free inheritance much more than a taxable one. Assuming you're going to teach your loved ones the saving, directing, and investing money strategies discussed here, you can be assured they'll put that tax-free cash to good use.

Roth IRAs for Kids

One of the best financially related gifts you can give your children is the gift of a Roth IRA. There is no age limit to contribute; however, earned income is required, and it must be legitimate. Paying your kid to cut the grass, for example, won't qualify.

If your child is under the age of 18, a custodial Roth IRA is required, but the custodial designation is easily removed once they're older.

As a bonus, their contribution will more than likely qualify for a full saver's tax credit, potentially wiping out any tax liability they might have incurred from their income.

Encourage their savings by matching any contributions they make. Or just give them the money to contribute.

Can you imagine what a few thousand invested

wisely at age 18 will look like several decades from now? A huge wad of tax-free dough, that's what. It's also a great way to teach your kids about investing. Once those tax-free earnings start piling up, they'll want to learn more.

Traditional IRA

A traditional IRA is a place to contribute and/or stash your pre-tax money. Remember, in the IRA world you've got to "keep 'em separated": Pre-tax money goes into a traditional IRA, Roth contributions to a Roth IRA. This is unlike 401(k)-type plans that accept both flavors. There are several ways to fund your traditional IRA.

Deductible Contributions

If your employer doesn't offer a retirement plan, you can make a deductible contribution to a traditional IRA up to the maximum yearly traditional IRA contribution limits, however high your income.

If you have a retirement plan at work, you can still make a deductible contribution to a traditional IRA, but only if you're under the AGI limits set by Uncle Sam. An additional traditional IRA AGI schedule determines your eligibility to make a deductible traditional IRA contribution if your spouse is covered but you're not:

You or Your Spouse are Covered by an Employer Retirement Plan 2025			
You're Covered			
If you file as...	**No Deduction**	**Partial Deduction**	**Full Deduction**
Single or Head of Household	$89,000 or more	$79,000-$89,000	$79,000 or less
Married Filing Jointly	$146,00 or more	$126,000-146,000	126,000 or less
Married Filling Separate	$10,000 or more	Less than $10,000	n/a
Your Spouse is Covered			
If you file as...	**No Deduction**	**Partial Deduction**	**Full Deduction**
Married Filing Jointly	$246,000 or more	$236,000-$246,000	$236,000 or less
Married Filling Separate	$10,000 or more	Less than $10,000	n/a

Nondeductible Contributions

Regardless of a high income or the presence of a work-related retirement plan, anyone can make what's known as a nondeductible traditional IRA contribution up to the IRA contribution limits for the year. This is the equivalent of making after-tax contributions to a 401(k)-type plan.

Even though your traditional IRA can't house your Roth money, it can contain both deductible and nondeductible contributions. If kept in the account until age 59 1/2, distributions of pre-tax contributions and associated earnings would be fully taxable, while only the earnings portion of the distribution of nondeductible funds would be taxable (since you paid tax on the principal in the year of the contribution).

If you're not subject to the IRS pro-rata rule, you can execute a backdoor Roth conversion of the nondeductible contribution and have your earnings accrue tax-free instead.

Rollovers

A rollover is a tax and penalty-free exchange from one plan to another. If you still have money with an old employer's plan, one of your options is rolling your pre-tax contributions and earnings into a traditional IRA and Roth contributions into a Roth IRA. Another is to roll that old employer plan money into your next employer's plan.

Most employer plans prohibit rollovers while you are gainfully employed. However, once you cease employment or reach age 59 1/2, those funds become portable, and rollovers are allowed.

If you are dissatisfied with the current custodian of your traditional IRA, you can roll it over into another traditional IRA anytime with no tax or penalty. If you want, you can have multiple traditional IRAs, but you still can only contribute aggregately up to the yearly contribution maximum.

Required Minimum Distributions (RMDs)

RMDs can be brutal. They kick in once you reach your mid-seventies and include not only money in your traditional IRAs but pre-tax contributions and earnings from employer plans too.

If you've done a good job saving for retirement over the years, that RMD can be a soberingly large number, especially after it's added to the rest of your income. And that's to say nothing about the government raising tax rates, which seems inevitable.

RMDs are all about Uncle Sam's lust for that taxable money sitting in your pre-tax accounts. He's been waiting for it a long time, and he's going to make sure he gets it by attaching a 25% penalty on the amount you were supposed to take out. That's down from a 50% penalty previously.

The Secure Act 2.0 was passed by Congress and signed into law at the end of 2022. Its provisions increased the starting age for RMDs to 73 for 2023, rising to age 75 in 2033.

Uncle Sam will supply you with your RMD percentage each year and will continue to do so until all your pre-tax money is exhausted, or you die, whichever comes first.

The percentage that first year, and every year thereafter, is based on predicted longevity statistics from actuarial tables and your filing status. That's the percentage you and other individuals like you need to take out.

This could result in a tax problem just when you need it least—in the latter years of your retirement. I warned you RMDs can be brutal!

Do you anticipate generating a bunch of earnings from your contributions? The more earnings you generate, the more motivated you should be to suck it up and avoid the problem of higher taxes and RMDs by going Roth rather than traditional. Young people have long time horizons for investment and can expect large amounts of tax-free earnings. So do savvy investors who expect above-average returns.

Traditional IRA to Roth IRA Conversion

Uncle Sam loves it when you convert money from your traditional IRA or employer-sponsored plan into a Roth IRA. It results in more immediate tax revenue. He especially loves it if you convert money and you're in a higher tax bracket.

Just remember that every penny converted is added to the rest of your ordinary income for the year and taxed as ordinary income. This results in higher taxes, potentially much higher, for you in the calendar year of the conversion.

Be smart about conversions. A good time for a conversion might be when you have a lower income because of a sabbatical, pandemic, or other unpaid time off. Other reasons might be worries about higher tax rates or a projected high RMD amount.

I admit to making a 5-figure conversion from my traditional IRA to my Roth IRA recently. "Why did you do that?" my accountant is bound to ask at tax time next year. All he sees are the negatives, which I admit shouldn't be overlooked. But I argue that his viewpoint is a bit shortsighted. It's best to look at the negatives as well as the positives through the eyes of your unique situation. That's the only way to make the right call as your own best money manager.

Roth Conversion Negatives

- **Adds to Ordinary Income** – More ordinary income means more tax. That means less disposable income.

- **Potentially Higher Healthcare Costs** – Health insurance premiums through the Affordable Care Act, Medicaid, and Medicare are based on your ordinary income for the year. That extra income from the conversion could cause an increase in your premiums.

- **Could Have Lower Taxes if You Wait** – If you're retired when you start distributions from your tax-advantaged account, might you be in a lower tax bracket when you take the money out rather than the higher one you're in now?

Roth Conversion Positives

- **No Income or Conversion Limits** – You can convert an unlimited amount of money from your traditional IRA to a Roth IRA in any given calendar year. Plus, there are no Roth IRA income limits like there are when determining your Roth IRA contribution limits.

- **Higher After-Tax Rate of Return** – Money

earned post-conversion is tax-free. The more money you earn, the bigger your after-tax advantage.

- **Take Advantage of Volatility** – You can convert money anytime during the calendar year. I decided to convert when I did because the stock market was down substantially, nearly 20%. If I had instead converted earlier in the year before the big drop-off, I'd potentially have to pay tax on a part of the conversion I would no longer have. Since I'm hopeful the market will eventually bounce back, that could be an extra boon to my rate of return. Of course, it could go down another 20% too. No one knows. That's why it's so hard to try and time the market.

- **Minimizes Required Minimum Distributions** (RMDs) – Do you have a sizable chunk of change invested in taxable tax-advantaged accounts? Come your mid-seventies, RMDs kick in. Estimate your RMDs and add them to your projected social security checks (85%), pensions, dividends, interest, and other taxable income. If that figure is big enough to choke a horse, you might be facing a tax problem in the latter years of your retirement. Converting money, hopefully when the stock market and your income is lower, is one way to reduce the size of those RMDs.

- **Impervious to Future Tax Hikes** – One assumption a lot of folks make is they'll be in a lower tax bracket when they take distributions from their taxable retirement accounts. Not so fast. The current low tax rates we enjoy are due to expire after the tax year 2025. I hate to say this, but if you're planning to take distributions after that date, I'm guessing federal and if applicable state and local taxes are going to be way higher, not the same or lower than they are now.

- **A Great Way to Pass Along Tax-Free Wealth** – I've decided to save my Roth money till last, to not tap it until all my traditional and regular taxable accounts have been exhausted, assuming I live that long. I reason that if things start to get even crazier, my best shot at keeping pace is with tax-free earnings and principal. And if I don't make it to that point, I know my heirs will be receiving tax-free cash rather than the taxable variety in their inheritance. And it's a legal way to avoid probate too. Just be sure to properly complete the beneficiary statement that comes with your Roth IRA.

"Filling Out" Your Tax Bracket

Have empathy for your future self with a strategy I call filling out your bracket. I'm talking about your tax bracket, not your NCAA basketball picks. Convert just enough money from your traditional IRA to a Roth IRA to "fill out" the tax bracket you find yourself in when you calculate your taxes.

This takes forethought since the deadline for converting money is now the end of the calendar year. Plus, you can't undo the conversion as you could before.

For example, say you are a single filer in 2025 and want to convert some money, and you're comfortable that your estimate of $43,000 in taxable income for the tax year 2025 is accurate. Since you're still thousands below the next highest bracket, you should be able to safely convert $3,000 sometime during 2025 without making the big jump from 12% to 22% tax on the amount converted.

If you're on the younger side, how much tax-free

earnings will that $3,000 generate? I'm betting a boatload. Be nice to your future self and provide them with lots of tax-free cash. This is yet another way to boost your after-tax return.

Health Savings Account

A Health Saving Account (HSA) can be used in association with a certain type of health insurance to help save you money on your out-of-pocket medical expenses. However, because of all the tax breaks you get with an HSA, you may want to consider using it as your number one tool for building wealth.

First the tax breaks. The following assumes a "qualified distribution":

A Quadruple Tax Break!

1. tax deduction on contributions

2. tax-free distribution of contributions

3. tax-free distribution of earnings

4. no payroll tax deducted on contributions (assuming contributions are made via employee payroll deduction)

With pre-tax contributions to a 401(k)-type plan or traditional IRA, you enjoy #1, with Roth contributions #3. With an HSA, you get all four!

Everything else being equal, you'll enjoy a higher after-tax rate of return in an HSA than any other account on the planet. Why not use some or all your HSA contributions to build your wealth faster?

Choosing Health Insurance

You get your health insurance through your employer, or your spouse's employer, or you purchase it privately or through the exchanges. However you receive it, you must choose an HSA-compatible health insurance plan to be able to contribute to an HSA. In health insurance parlance, that means choosing what's known as a *high-deductible health plan.*

As the name implies, this healthcare option comes with a higher deductible than the other plans. This is in exchange for lower monthly premium payments and higher out-of-pocket healthcare costs, as compared to lower deductible plans when you receive care during the plan year.

That's why investing some or all the funds in your HSA isn't for everyone: You must choose a high-deductible health plan to be able to contribute to an HSA. Still, the tax advantages may offset those costs and then some.

Invest Your HSA

Yes, you can invest some or all your HSA funds. If this interests you, the way I see it, you've got three choices as to how to best utilize your HSA. Choose the investing option that's right for you.

Option #1

Estimate your yearly medical expenses for the coming year and deposit that amount in your HSA's least risky account option. This is usually your default option and may be a non-interest-bearing account or maybe a money market/savings type account. If you're lucky and your employer contributes on your behalf, you may not need to contribute any extra.

Whenever a qualified medical expense occurs during the year, reimburse yourself with tax-free cash from your HSA. Even though this option is not a wealth-builder, you still are saving money on your taxes. Plus, any unused funds are available for your use next year or any year thereafter, even if you move on to another employer or have different health insurance.

Option #2

Make the maximum allowable contribution ($4,300 single/$8,550 family for 2025) to your HSA every year you choose a high-deductible plan. Put the funds you anticipate needing for medical expenses for the coming year into your HSA's default account option. Aggressively invest whatever is left over.

If you have employer-sponsored insurance, your employer chooses the custodian of your HSA for you. It's possible that HSA custodian doesn't offer investment options or offers only lousy investment options. That's not a problem.

Transfer the investment portion of your contributions to an HSA of your choosing that has high-performing funds and low fees. HSAs are individual accounts, so your employer has no say as to what you do with your HSA funds.

You can even transfer funds your employer deposited on your behalf as soon as they hit your account. The IRS, by the way, has no problem with you having multiple HSAs, just like it's cool to have multiple IRAs.

If you or your spouse don't have employer-sponsored health insurance, you must get it yourself privately or over the exchanges. Assuming you signed up for an HSA-compatible health plan, you get to choose your own HSA custodian. I like the high-performing, low-cost HSA options offered by Fidelity®.

Option #3

As with option #2, make the maximum allowable contribution ($4,300 single/$8,550 family for 2025) to your HSA. Instead of allocating money for your use during the current plan year, with this option, you invest all of it.

By utilizing this maximize your earnings strategy year after year, you can rack up a staggering amount of tax-free bank, to say nothing of the yearly tax deduction. Of course, with this option, you need to pay your medical expenses out-of-pocket with after-tax funds.

That means your medical expenses each year will be higher because you're not cashing in your tax break. You're saving it for later.

If you can afford this option, you're betting that the utility you gain from your investments is greater than using the money immediately. With all the tax breaks you get and your well-thought-out investment plan, that shouldn't be hard to do.

Save those unreimbursed medical receipts. They act as tickets for tax-free distributions from your HSA any time you need the money in the future. There is no time limit as far as reimbursement goes.

As an example, say you go with option #3 this year, but next year you get a new job and elect health insurance that is not HSA compatible. Assuming you saved your medical receipts from last year, you can use them to make a tax-free withdrawal from your HSA in the current year or any year thereafter.

Personally, I'm resisting tapping that tax-free cash until later. That way I can rack up even more tax-free earnings. Just make sure you're saving the paperwork that's needed if you happen to get audited. I recommend scanning and electronic storage, especially if you're saving medical receipts for years if not decades like I am.

Qualifying Distribution Defined

Distributions must be "qualified" to be tax and penalty-free. Qualified means you are reimbursing yourself for qualified medical expenses incurred by you, your spouse, and other dependents as defined by Uncle Sam.

Qualified medical expenses include all deductibles, co-pays, co-insurance, and certain over-the-counter medicines and supplies.

In response to the Covid crisis, the list of qualified expenses (*https://www.irs.gov/pub/irs-pdf/p502.pdf*) has been greatly expanded and now includes sunscreen, skin moisturizers, and menstrual products, among others.

The list does not, however, include your share of your health insurance premium. Once you turn age 65 and sign up for Medicare, however, withdraws to pay for your Parts B and D premiums *are* considered qualified. With the 2025 Part B Medicare standard premium at $185 a month, that's a substantial expense you'll have covered.

Be aware no double-dipping is allowed. If a medical expense was previously taken as a deduction on a past tax return or used previously as reimbursement from an HSA, FSA, HRA, or another tax-advantaged healthcare-related account, it can't be used again.

Future Medical Expenses
What if you choose Option #3 and you enjoy a best-case scenario: You and your family are so healthy you barely touched any of your HSA contributions and earnings by the time you reach age 65. One can only wish!

Once you reach age 65, the brutal 20% penalty for withdrawing unqualified distributions is lifted. You can now withdraw money and use it for anything you wish, but you will have to pay tax on it at ordinary income tax rates if it's not qualified.

That's still pretty good, much like a qualified withdrawal from a traditional IRA. Not so fast, though. You may want to keep that money hanging around a little longer.

Long-Term Care Needs

If you or your spouse require long-term care for an extended period, it could be devastating to your finances. Long-term care is custodial care and is barely covered by Medicare. In many areas of the country, 24/7 custodial care tops $100,000 per year.

You can purchase long-term care insurance to protect against this peril but beware of the pricey premiums. Plus, if you don't need long-term care, which hopefully you won't, it's not like you get any of those premiums back.

If you have a long-term care insurance policy, some, or all (depending on your age) of your premium payments are considered qualified HSA expenses. That helps offset those pricey premiums somewhat.

Your other alternative is to self-insure yourself against this potential peril. Long-term care expenses are HSA-qualified. Even if you don't need long-term care, it is more than likely your medical expenses will be higher in your latter years, so it's always nice to have that extra cushion.

Stack the Deck

This is just another way you can get a leg-up in the dog-eat-dog world of Wall Street. It might not seem like much, but over time these amounts you're saving and investing in a tax-advantaged nature here and there really add up. It's nice to have the deck stacked in your favor for a change.

Pre-Paid Tuition Plan

Almost every state used to offer a pre-paid tuition plan, but now it's down to less than a dozen. You basically pre-pay tuition for a state-run college or university now. Your younger student is then able to attend an in-state college or university tuition-free in the future, with the state government making up the difference in tuition hikes with their investments.

A select number of plans allow your student to attend university outside your state of residence, but most don't. Besides the restrictions as to where your student goes to school, the rub with these plans is that you're entrusting your money to a state-run municipality.

I'm sure the powers that be in your state of residence will make savvy investments with your money and everything works out (written with a bit of sarcasm). Once there were many, now there are few: Most states disbanded their pre-paid tuition plans shortly after the 2008 stock investing debacle due to improper money management.

Check out all your possibilities. If your state of residence offers one of these plans, maybe it's right for you. Just be sure to check out your 529 options as well.

529 Plan

Think of 529 plans as Roth IRAs for education. Like a Roth IRA, there is no federal tax deduction on contributions, but all future earnings accrue tax-free. The catch is, that to make tax-free withdrawals, the money must be used to pay for the educational expenses of the named beneficiary of the plan.

Educational expenses include not just tuition, books, and fees, but lodging and other living expenses too. There is no limit on the amount you can withdraw per year for higher education expenses, but for K-12 expenses there is a $10,000 limit per year per beneficiary.

The beneficiary is the person earmarked to receive the funds, whether it be you, your spouse, kids, or grandkids. You, the owner of the account, can change the beneficiary once a year to anyone even remotely related to the original beneficiary.

Like Roth IRAs, it's best to try and contribute to these accounts early on. That maximizes your tax advantage and your tax-free earnings.

Much like the other tax-advantaged accounts we've discussed, you can create a customized investment plan using the investment options of your chosen custodian.

Like pre-paid tuition plans, 529 plans are run by state municipalities. Your custodian could be Pennsylvania, Michigan, California, or another state. You can invest in any state's plan, regardless of residence or where the beneficiary eventually attends school.

If your state of residence has a state income tax, check to see if they offer a state tax deduction on state tax for residents. Some do and some don't. That would be the only tax advantage to investing in your state's plan over another state's plan.

Like employer-sponsored plans, the quality of

offerings can vary greatly from state to state. Some offer enlightened investment offerings with high returns and low fees. Others offer the equivalent of a 401(k)-dog plan, so don't blindly go with your own state's plan. Do some research.

You can contribute yearly up to the 529 plan contribution limit, and there are no AGI limitations. Multiple 529 Plans can be set up for a single beneficiary, so parents, grandparents, and anyone else who wants to contribute to your student's education is free to do so.

Thanks to the Secure Act 2.0, beneficiaries of 529s can convert unused balances to their Roth IRAs via a 529 to Roth IRA rollover. Restrictions, including the 529 is at least 15 years old, apply.

Another big change was how distributions from non-parental 529s count on the Free Application for Federal Student Aid (FASFA).

Before recent legislation, grandparents and other non-parental 529 benefactors' efforts to help would often backfire. Until 2024, distributions were counted as income to students on the beneficiary's FASFA. That extra income often reduced the federal aid the beneficiary was due to receive. That's no longer the case.

Money withdrawn from a non-spousal 529 no longer counts as income to the beneficiary on the FASFA. Plus, it won't count as an asset on the FASFA either. This rule change now makes a 529 plan opened and funded by benefactors other than the parents the ideal college savings strategy.

Well-healed grandparents may now even consider overfunding their 529 plan on purpose. That way, they can help with their grandkid's education *and* eventually jumpstart their journey to financial independence too with yearly 529 to Roth IRA rollovers.

Nerdwallet, SavingForCollege, and The Motley Fool are good sources of information on 529 plans. So are the websites maintained by the state-run plans.

Educational Savings Account

Educational Savings Accounts, or ESAs, have AGI limits and a contribution limit of $2,000 per year. If you're under the ESA income limits and you don't want to invest more than $2,000 per year for education, an ESA could be a good choice.

ESA Income Limits			
Filing Method	**Max Allowed**	**Partial Allowed**	**None**
Single, married filing separately, head of household	MAGI less than $95,000	MAGI equal to or greater than $95,000 but less than or equal to $110,000	MAGI greater than $110,000
Married filing jointly	MAGI less than $190,000	MAGI equal to or greater than $190,000 but less than/equal to $220,000	MAGI greater than $220,000

Unlike 529 plans, there is an overall limit of $2,000 of contributions per year, not per account. There can be multiple ESAs saving for the same beneficiary, but aggregate contributions can't exceed the $2,000 limit per year.

The big advantage of an ESA is you don't have to deal with a state municipality as your custodian like with a 529 plan. Many investment companies that offer IRAs and brokerage services offer ESAs. Choose one that offers low fees and excellent investment options.

Be Your Own Best Money Manager

Never stop learning. Proper money management is just one way you can help yourself live a fuller, more satisfying life. I wish you the best. Stay prosperous and safe.

###

Appendix A: Consolidated Examples

In the Risk Management Strategies section, I used the same three short-, intermediate-, and long-term goals as examples at the end of each respective chapter. Appendix B combines the risky to not-so-risky ratio and the dynamic diversification examples together for your convenience.

Example #1

In example #1, you're creating an investment plan for a short-term goal of two years. The risky to not-so-risky ratios and dynamic diversification for ultra-conservative and super-aggressive portfolios are as follows:

Plan Year ~ Conservative Ratio ~ Aggressive Ratio

Plan Year **1: Conservative investor** – 100% not-so-risky: all in short-term CDs and FDIC-insured high-yield savings/money market accounts ~ **Aggressive investor** – 100% not-so-risky: 50% short-term bond fund, 50% short-term CDs and FDIC-insured high-yield savings/money market accounts

Plan Year **2: Conservative investor** – 100% not-so-risky: all in short-term CDs and FDIC-insured high-yield savings/money market accounts ~ **Aggressive investor** – 100% not-so-risky: all in short-term CDs and FDIC-insured high-yield savings/money market accounts

Example #2

Example #2 is a medium-term educational goal of 10 years (for an 8-year-old) with a 4-year distribution period. The risky to not-so-risky ratios and dynamic diversification for ultra-conservative and super-aggressive portfolios are as follows:

Plan Year **1: Conservative investor** – 25% risky: 18% US large cap, 5% US mid-small cap, 2% international 75% not-so-risky: all in total bond market fund ~ **Aggressive investor** – 75% risky: 30% US large cap, 30% US mid-small cap, 15% international 25% not-so-risky: all in total bond market fund

Plan Year **2: Conservative investor** – 23% risky: 18% US large cap, 4% US mid-small cap, 1% international 77% not-so-risky: all in total bond market fund ~ **Aggressive investor** – 70% risky: 30% US large cap, 28% US mid-small cap, 12% international 30% not-so-risky: all in total bond market fund

Plan Year **3**: **Conservative investor** – 21% risky: 18% US large cap, 3% US mid-small cap 79% not-so-risky: all in total bond market fund ~ **Aggressive investor** – 65% risky: 30% US large cap, 25% US mid-small cap, 10% international 35% not-so-risky: all in total bond market fund

Plan Year **4**: **Conservative investor** – 18% risky: 16% US large cap, 2% US mid-small cap 82% not-so-risky: all in total bond market fund ~ **Aggressive investor** – 60% risky: 30% US large cap, 23% US mid-small cap, 7% international 40% not-so-risky: all in total bond market fund

Plan Year **5**: **Conservative investor** – 15% risky: 15% US large cap 85% not-so-risky: all in total bond market fund ~ **Aggressive investor** – 50% risky: 30% US large cap, 18% US mid-small cap, 2% international 50% not-so-risky: all in total bond market fund

Plan Year **6**: **Conservative investor** – 12% risky: 12% US large cap 88% not-so-risky: 75% total bond market fund, 13% short-term bond fund ~ **Aggressive investor** – 45% risky: 30% US large cap, 15% US mid-small cap 55% not-so-risky: all in total bond market fund

Plan Year **7**: **Conservative investor** – 9% risky: 9% US large cap 91% not-so-risky: 60% total bond

market fund, 31% short-term bond fund ~
Aggressive investor – 40% risky: 30% US large cap, 10% US mid-small cap 60% not-so-risky: 55% total bond market fund, 5% short-term bond fund.

Plan Year **8**: **Conservative investor** – 6% risky: 6% US large cap 94% not-so-risky: 45% total bond market fund, 49% short-term bond fund ~
Aggressive investor – 35% risky: 30% US large cap, 5% US mid-small cap 65% not-so-risky: 50% total bond market fund, 15% short-term bond fund

Plan Year **9**: **Conservative investor** – 3% risky: 3% US large cap 97% not-so-risky: 25% total bond market fund, 52% short-term bond fund, 20% mixture of money markets and CDs that carry FDIC insurance ~ **Aggressive investor** – 30% risky: 30% US large cap 70% not-so-risky: 40% total bond market fund, 30% short-term bond fund

Plan Year **10**: **Conservative investor** – 0% risky 100% not-so-risky: 5% total bond market fund, 45% short-term bond fund, 50% mixture of money markets and CDs that carry FDIC insurance ~
Aggressive investor – 25% risky: 25% US large cap 75% not-so-risky: 25% total bond market fund, 30% short-term bond fund, 20% mixture of money markets and CDs that carry FDIC insurance and ultra-short bond funds

off to college

Plan Year **11**: **Conservative investor** – 0% risky 100% not-so-risky: 20% short-term bond fund, 80% mixture of money markets and CDs that carry FDIC insurance **Aggressive investor** – 20% risky: 20% US large cap 80% not-so-risky: 40% short-term bond fund, 40% mixture of money markets and CDs that carry FDIC insurance and ultra-short bond funds

Plan Year **12**: **Conservative investor** – 0% risky 100% not-so-risky: 10% short-term bond fund, 90% mixture of money markets and CDs that carry FDIC insurance ~ **Aggressive investor** – 10% risky: 10% US large cap 90% not-so-risky: 35% short-term bond fund, 55% mixture of money markets and CDs that carry FDIC insurance

Plan Year **13**: **Conservative investor** – 0% risky 100% not-so-risky: mixture of money markets and CDs that carry FDIC insurance ~ **Aggressive investor** – 5% risky: 5% US large cap 95% not-so-risky: 35% short-term bond fund, 65% mixture of money markets and CDs that carry FDIC insurance

Plan Year **14**: **Conservative investor** – 0% risky 100% not-so-risky: mixture of money markets and CDs that carry FDIC insurance ~ **Aggressive**

investor – 0% risky 100% not-so-risky: mixture of money markets and CDs that carry FDIC insurance

Example #3

Example #3 is a long-term retirement goal of 25 years. The risky to not-so-risky ratios and dynamic diversification for an ultra-conservative and super-aggressive portfolio are as follows:

Plan Year **1**: **Conservative investor** – 70% risky: 40% US large cap, 15% US mid-small cap, 15% international 30% not-so-risky: 30% total bond market fund ~ **Aggressive investor** – 99% risky: 39% US large cap, 30% US mid-small cap, 30% international 1% not-so-risky: all in total bond market fund

Plan Year **2**: **Conservative investor** – 68% risky: 40% US large cap, 14% US mid-small cap, 14% international 32% not-so-risky: 32% total bond market fund ~ **Aggressive investor** – 99% risky: 39% US large cap, 30% US mid-small cap, 30% international 1% not-so-risky: all in total bond market fund

Plan Year **3**: **Conservative investor** – 66% risky: 40% US large cap, 14% US mid-small cap, 12% international 34% not-so-risky: 34% total bond market fund ~ **Aggressive investor** – 98% risky: 39% US large cap, 30% US mid-small cap, 29% international 2% not-so-risky: all in total bond market fund

Plan Year **4**: **Conservative investor** – 64% risky: 40% US large cap, 13% US mid-small cap, 11% international 36% not-so-risky: all in total bond market fund ~ **Aggressive investor** – 98% risky: 39% US large cap, 30% US mid-small cap, 29% international 2% not-so-risky: all in total bond market fund

Plan Year **5**: **Conservative investor** – 62% risky: 40% US large cap, 12% US mid-small cap, 10% international 38% not-so-risky: all in total bond market fund ~ **Aggressive investor** – 96% risky: 39% US large cap, 30% US mid-small cap, 27% international 4% not-so-risky: all in total bond market fund

Plan Year **6**: **Conservative investor** – 60% risky: 40% US large cap, 12% US mid-small cap, 8% international 40% not-so-risky: all in total bond market fund ~ **Aggressive investor** – 94% risky: 39% US large cap, 29% US mid-small cap, 26% international 6% not-so-risky: all in total bond market fund

Plan Year **7**: **Conservative investor** – 58% risky:

40% US large cap, 11% US mid-small cap, 7% international 42% not-so-risky: all in total bond market fund ~ **Aggressive investor** – 92% risky: 39% US large cap, 29% US mid-small cap, 24% international 8% not-so-risky: all in total bond market fund

Plan Year **8: Conservative investor** – 56% risky: 40% US large cap, 10% US mid-small cap, 6% international 44% not-so-risky: all in total bond market fund ~ **Aggressive investor** – 90% risky: 39% US large cap, 29% US mid-small cap, 22% international 10% not-so-risky: all in total bond market fund

Plan Year **9: Conservative investor** – 54% risky: 40% US large cap, 10% US mid-small cap, 4% international 46% not-so-risky: all in total bond market fund ~ **Aggressive investor** – 88% risky: 39% US large cap, 29% US mid-small cap, 20% international 12% not-so-risky: all in total bond market fund

Plan Year **10: Conservative investor** – 52% risky: 40% US large cap, 10% US mid-small cap, 2% international 48% not-so-risky: all in total bond market fund ~ **Aggressive investor** – 86% risky: 39% US large cap, 29% US mid-small cap, 18% international 14% not-so-risky: all in total bond market fund

Plan Year **11**: **Conservative investor** – 50% risky: 40% US large cap, 9% US mid-small cap 1% international 50% not-so-risky: all in total bond market fund ~ **Aggressive investor** – 84% risky: 39% US large cap, 28% US mid-small cap, 17% international 16% not-so-risky: all in total bond market fund

Plan Year **12**: **Conservative investor** – 48% risky: 40% US large cap, 8% US mid-small cap 52% not-so-risky: all in total bond market fund ~ **Aggressive investor** – 82% risky: 39% US large cap, 28% US mid-small cap, 15% international 18% not-so-risky: all in total bond market fund

Plan Year **13**: **Conservative investor** – 46% risky: 40% US large cap, 6% US mid-small cap 54% not-so-risky: all in total bond market fund ~ **Aggressive investor** – 80% risky: 39% US large cap, 27% US mid-small cap, 14% international 20% not-so-risky: all in total bond market fund

Plan Year **14**: **Conservative investor** – 44% risky: 40% US large cap, 4% US mid-small cap 56% not-so-risky: all in total bond market fund ~ **Aggressive investor** – 79% risky: 39% US large cap, 27% US mid-small cap, 13% international 21% not-so-risky: all in total bond market fund

Plan Year **15**: **Conservative investor** – 42% risky:

40% US large cap, 2% US mid-small cap 58% not-so-risky: all in total bond market fund ~
Aggressive investor – 78% risky: 39% US large cap, 27% US mid-small cap, 12% international 22% not-so-risky: all in total bond market fund

Plan Year **16**: **Conservative investor** – 40% risky: 40% US large cap 60% not-so-risky: 55% total bond market fund, 5% short-term bond fund ~
Aggressive investor – 77% risky: 39% US large cap, 27% US mid-small cap, 11% international 23% not-so-risky: all in total bond market fund

Plan Year **17**: **Conservative** investor – 38% risky: 38% US large cap 62% not-so-risky: 50% total bond market fund 12% short-term bond fund ~
Aggressive investor – 76% risky: 39% US large cap, 27% US mid-small cap, 10% international 24% not-so-risky: all in total bond market fund

Plan Year **18**: **Conservative investor** – 36% risky: 36% US large cap 64% not-so-risky: 45% total bond market fund, 19% short-term bond fund ~
Aggressive investor – 75% risky: 39% US large cap, 26% US mid-small cap, 10% international 25% not-so-risky: all in total bond market fund

Plan Year **19**: **Conservative** investor – 34% risky: 34% US large cap 66% not-so-risky:40% total bond market fund, 26% short-term bond fund ~

Aggressive investor – 74% risky: 39% US large cap, 26% US mid-small cap, 9% international 26% not-so-risky: all in total bond market fund

Plan Year **20**: **Conservative investor** – 32% risky: 32% US large cap 68% not-so-risky: 35% total bond market fund, 33% short-term bond fund ~ **Aggressive investor** – 73% risky: 39% US large cap, 26% US mid-small cap, 8% international 27% not-so-risky: all in total bond market fund

Plan Year **21**: **Conservative investor** – 30% risky: 30% US large cap 70% not-so-risky: 30% total bond market fund, 40% short-term bond fund ~ **Aggressive investor** – 72% risky: 39% US large cap, 25% US mid-small cap, 8% international 28% not-so-risky: all in total bond market fund

Plan Year **22**: **Conservative investor** – 29% risky: 29% US large cap 71% not-so-risky: 25% total bond market fund, 46% short-term bond fund ~ **Aggressive investor** – 70% risky: 39% US large cap, 23% US mid-small cap, 8% international 30% not-so-risky: all in total bond market fund

Plan Year **23**: **Conservative investor** – 27% risky: 27% US large cap 73% not-so-risky: 20% total bond market fund 48% short-term bond fund 5% mixture of money markets and CDs that carry FDIC insurance ~ **Aggressive investor** – 68%

risky: 39% US large cap, 21% US mid-small cap, 8% international 32% not-so-risky: all in total bond market fund

Plan Year **24**: **Conservative investor** – 26% risky: 26% US large cap 74% not-so-risky: 15% total bond market fund, 49% short-term bond fund, 10% mixture of money markets and CDs that carry FDIC insurance ~ **Aggressive investor** – 66% risky: 39% US large cap, 19% US mid-small cap, 8% international 34% not-so-risky: all in total bond market fund

Plan Year **25**: **Conservative investor** – 25% risky: 25% US large cap 75% not-so-risky: 15% total bond market fund, 45% short term bond fund, 15% mixture of money markets and CDs that carry FDIC insurance ~ **Aggressive investor** – 65% risky: 39% US large cap, 18% US mid-small cap, 8% international 35% not-so-risky: 30% total bond market fund, 5% mixture of money markets and CDs that carry FDIC insurance

retirement date

Once you reach your retirement date and start to live off your savings, there are many variables to consider when setting both your risky to not-so-risky ratios and dynamic diversification percentages for your distribution period. They include your health, the health of your spouse, the size of your projected RMD payments, and the size of your remaining savings.

That's why it's a good idea to reassess your numbers on your rebalancing and reassessing dates. And even though circumstances may change, fill in your distribution years now too, just as you did for your pre-retirement years.

Plan Year **26**: **Conservative investor** – 24% risky: 24% US large cap 76% not-so-risky: 14% total bond market fund, 40% short-term bond fund, 22% mixture of money markets and CDs that carry FDIC insurance ~ **Aggressive investor** – 65% risky: 39% US large cap, 18% US mid-small cap, 8% international 35% not-so-risky: 30% total bond market fund, 5% mixture of money markets and CDs that carry FDIC insurance

Plan Year **27**: **Conservative investor** – 24% risky: 24% US large cap 76% not-so-risky: 14% total bond market fund, 40% short-term bond fund, 22% mixture of money markets and CDs that carry FDIC insurance ~ **Aggressive investor** – 65% risky: 39% US large cap, 18% US mid-small cap, 8% international 35% not-so-risky: 30% total bond market fund, 5% mixture of money markets and CDs that carry FDIC insurance

Plan Year **28**: **Conservative investor** – 23% risky: 23% US large cap 77% not-so-risky: 12% total bond market fund 40% short-term bond fund, 25% mixture of money markets and CDs that carry FDIC insurance ~ **Aggressive investor** – 64% risky: 39% US large cap, 17% US mid-small cap, 8% international 36% not-so-risky: 30% total bond market fund, 6% mixture of money markets and CDs that carry FDIC insurance

Plan Year **29**: **Conservative investor** – 23% risky: 23% US large cap 77% not-so-risky: 12% total bond market fund 40% short-term bond fund, 25% mixture of money markets and CDs that carry FDIC insurance ~ **Aggressive investor** – 63% risky: 39% US large cap, 16% US mid-small cap, 8% international 37% not-so-risky: 30% total bond market fund, 7% mixture of money markets and CDs that carry FDIC insurance

Plan Year **30**: **Conservative investor** – 22% risky: 22% US large cap 78% not-so-risky: 11% total bond market fund, 40% short-term bond fund, 27% mixture of money markets and CDs that carry FDIC insurance ~ **Aggressive investor** – 62% risky: 39% US large cap, 15% US mid-small cap, 8% international 38% not-so-risky: 30% total bond market fund, 8% mixture of money markets and CDs that carry FDIC insurance

Plan Year **31: Conservative investor** – 21% risky: 21% US large cap 79% not-so-risky: 10% total bond market fund, 40% short-term bond fund, **29%** *mixture of* money markets and CDs that carry FDIC insurance ~ **Aggressive investor** – 61% risky: 39% US large cap, 14% US mid-small cap, 8% international 39% not-so-risky: 30% total bond market fund, 9% mixture of money markets and CDs that carry FDIC insurance

Plan Year **32: Conservative investor** – 20% risky: 20% US large cap 80% not-so-risky: Maintain at least 2 years' worth of living expenses in those FDIC-insured super-safe investments with the rest going to a short-term bond fund ~ **Aggressive investor** – 60% risky: 39% US large cap, 14% US mid-small cap, 7% international 40% not-so-risky: Maintain at least 2 years' worth of living expenses in those FDIC-insured super-safe investments with the rest spread out between a short-term bond fund and total bond market fund

Plan Year **33: Conservative investor** – 20% risky: 20% US large cap 80% not-so-risky: Maintain at least 2 years' worth of living expenses in those FDIC-insured super-safe investments with the rest going to a short-term bond fund ~ **Aggressive investor** – 60% risky: 40% US large cap, 14% US mid-small cap, 6% international 40% not-so-risky:

Maintain at least 2 years' worth of living expenses in those FDIC-insured super-safe investments with the rest spread out between a short-term bond fund and total bond market fund

Plan Year **34: Conservative investor** – 20% risky: 20% US large cap 80% not-so-risky: Maintain at least 2 years' worth of living expenses in those FDIC-insured super-safe investments with the rest going to a short-term bond fund ~ **Aggressive investor** – 60% risky: 41% US large cap, 14% US mid-small cap, 5% international 40% not-so-risky: Maintain at least 2 years' worth of living expenses in those FDIC-insured super-safe investments with the rest spread out between a short-term bond fund and total bond market fund

Plan Year **35: Conservative investor** – 20% risky: 20% US large cap 80% not-so-risky: Maintain at least 2 years' worth of living expenses in those FDIC-insured super-safe investments with the rest going to a short-term bond fund ~ **Aggressive investor** – 60% risky: 43% US large cap, 13% US mid-small cap, 4% international 40% not-so-risky: Maintain at least 2 years' worth of living expenses in those FDIC-insured super-safe investments with the rest spread out between a short-term bond fund and total bond market fund

Plan Year **36: Conservative investor** – 20% risky:

20% US large cap 80% not-so-risky: Maintain at least 2 years' worth of living expenses in those FDIC-insured super-safe investments with the rest going to a short-term bond fund ~ **Aggressive investor** – 60% risky: 45% US large cap, 12% US mid-small cap, 3% international 40% not-so-risky: Maintain at least 2 years' worth of living expenses in those FDIC-insured super-safe investments with the rest spread out between a short-term bond fund and total bond market fund

Plan Year **37: Conservative investor** – 20% risky: 20% US large cap 80% not-so-risky: Maintain at least 2 years' worth of living expenses in those FDIC-insured super-safe investments with the rest going to a short-term bond fund ~ **Aggressive investor** – 60% risky: 46% US large cap, 12% US mid-small cap, 2% international 40% not-so-risky: Maintain at least 2 years' worth of living expenses in those FDIC-insured super-safe investments with the rest spread out between a short-term bond fund and total bond market fund

Plan Year **38: Conservative investor** – 20% risky: 20% US large cap 80% not-so-risky: Maintain at least 2 years' worth of living expenses in those FDIC-insured super-safe investments with the rest going to a short-term bond fund ~ **Aggressive investor** – 60% risky: 48% US large cap, 11% US mid-small cap, 1% international 40% not-so-risky: Maintain at least 2 years' worth of living expenses in those FDIC-insured super-safe investments with the rest spread out between a short-term bond fund and total bond market fund

Plan Year **39**: **Conservative investor** – 20% risky: 20% US large cap 80% not-so-risky: Maintain at least 2 years' worth of living expenses in those FDIC-insured super-safe investments with the rest going to a short-term bond fund ~ **Aggressive investor** – 60% risky: 49% US large cap, 11% US mid-small cap 40% not-so-risky: Maintain at least 2 years' worth of living expenses in those FDIC-insured super-safe investments with the rest spread out between a short-term bond fund and total bond market fund

Plan Year **40**: **Conservative investor** – 20% risky: 20% US large cap 80% not-so-risky: Maintain at least 2 years' worth of living expenses in those FDIC-insured super-safe investments with the rest going to a short-term bond fund ~ **Aggressive investor** – 60% risky: 50% US large cap, 10% US mid-small cap 40% not-so-risky: Maintain at least 2 years' worth of living expenses in those FDIC-insured super-safe investments with the rest spread out between a short-term bond fund and total bond market fund

Appendix B: References

"Active vs. passive investing: which approach offers better returns?" 2018. *Wharton Executive Education.* accessed June 21, 2022. https://executiveeducation.wharton.upenn.edu/thought-leadership/wharton-wealth-management-initiative/wmi-thought-leadership/active-vs-passive-investing-which-approach-offers-better-returns/.

Brock, Catherine. 2022. "The best investment, according to Warren Buffett, and how you can own it." *The Motley Fool.* September 11, 2022. https://www.fool.com/investing/2022/09/11/the-best-investment-according-to-warren-buffett-an/.

Haslem, John A., H. Kent Baker, and David M. Smith. 2008. "Performance and characteristics of actively managed retail equity mutual funds with diverse expense ratios." *SSRN Electronic Journal.* https://doi.org/10.2139/ssrn.1128983.

"Investment planning vol 2: investment risk & return," 2009. *CFP® Certification Professional Educational Program,* Greenwood Village, CO: College for Financial Planning.

"Investment planning vol 3: modern portfolio theory." 2009. *CFP® Certification Professional Educational Program*, Greenwood Village, CO: College for Financial Planning.

Israelsen, Craig. 2013. "Tale of the tape: value vs growth." *Financial Planning*, April 2013.

Wood, Gael. 2018. "If you don't write your goals down, you might not achieve them." *Massage Magazine*, 1 January 2018.

Tengler, Nancy. 2020. "Find that balance between growth, value stocks." *USA Today*, 1 June 2020.

Weil, Dan. n.d. "Got inflation blues? consider dividend stocks: Wharton's Siegel." *TheStreet*. Accessed 7 November 2022. https://www.thestreet.com/investing/inflation-dividend-stocks-siegel.

About Keith Dorney

Keith Dorney was a 2-time All-American offensive tackle at Penn State University from 1975-78. He also earned Academic All-American honors and was elected to the College Football Hall of Fame in 2005.

The 10th pick in the 1st round of the 1979 NFL draft, he was chosen by the Detroit Lions where he played his entire career. Dorney received numerous honors as a professional, including Pro Bowl, All-NFC, and team MVP honors, and served as team captain from 1983-1987.

Post-football, Dorney turned to writing and teaching. A memoir, *Black and Honolulu Blue* (September 2003–Triumph Books) was his first book.

While earning his MA in Teaching (University of San Francisco), Dorney's resume included teaching Juvenile Hall-sanctioned programs and high school English.

More recently Dorney turned to corporate training, informing employees of Google®, Microsoft®, Cisco Systems®, Roche®, and other Fortune 500 companies how to maximize employee benefits and reach financial independence sooner.

A Certified Financial Planner® since 2010, Dorney now writes and teaches full-time from his farm south of Sebastopol, California, where he and his wife Katherine raised their two kids and still reside.

When not writing or teaching, he enjoys hanging out in the garden and spending time with family and friends.

Detailed Table of Contents